# The Forbidden Book
# of Getting What You Want

or
Make the World Your Banquet Starting With a
Simmering Broth of Ambition

## by

# JK Ellis

Lulu, Inc.

First published 2008

Copyright © JK Ellis 2007

**ISBN:** 978-1-4357-0359-9

Cover Design by
www.ecoverexpert.com

Formatted using Open Office
Printed and bound in the United States of America
by Lulu, Inc.
www.Lulu.com

# Table Of Contents

## Dedication.

*To Robert Greene, author of* **48 Laws of Power** *and*
**33 Strategies of War**, *who read over a thousand books for me
so that I might learn to spiritualize everything and
treat life like a glorious campaign.*

*And*

*To my faithful djinn, familiar and constant companion, Dantalion, the
seventy-first spirit of the Goetia, "His Office is to teach all Arts and
Sciences unto any; and to declare the Secret Counsel of any one; for
he knoweth the Thoughts of all Men and Women, and can change them
at his Will. He can cause Love, and show the Similitude of any person,
and show the same by a Vision, let them be in what part of the World
they Will."*

# Introduction

There are a few things you will notice as you read this book. The least of which is that I've made a conscious effort to **never** write a sentence with a word beginning with "I." This has been a much harder task than you might think but it was done with several intentions in mind. Firstly, there exists my personal distaste for overt bragging; I've avoided the pronoun "I" at the beginning of any sentence. A second reason is an exercise in INTENT. Some people call it "will". Others call it "intent". What "It" is, is the ability to make something happen simply because you choose to.

Both intent and intentions play a huge role in everyone's lives. They have a decided significance in determining whether people get what they want or not.

The word intent is defined in law as the planning and desire to perform an act. That definition works best of all for enhancing our understanding of intent in terms of everyday living.

Another definition for intent you will come across when you look the word up online, at least two, in fact, refer to intent as something of a spiritual state.

One website glossary defines intent as "the single most causal event in all action, creation, destruction, and change at all levels of existence. That component of consciousness which gives rise to all forms. The means by which the Will of God and Natural Law is manifest. The essence and source of motivation".[1]

We are attempting to deal with a concept that involves both conscious and deliberate thought. We are addressing a subconscious and spiritual form that impacts forces in the universe.

Now that we have a general idea of the definition, let's take a look at a famous example of intent. Believe it or not, this concept, this notion, has occupied quite a significant place in the collective conscious of mankind.

Shakespeare, for example, presents to us with a classic example of the power of intent in his history play, *Henry IV Part 2*. One scene in particular provides an inspiring demonstration of the power of intention. The scene depicts the death of one king and the

---

1      (http://www.eoni.com/-visionquest/library/glossary.html)

succession of his son. The intent of the future Henry V of England is, mainifested at his father's death bed, that strongly suggests the overpowering nature of this process of intending to do something on both a conscious and subconscious level.

Maybe you know something about British History, or if you happen to be a Shakespeare buff, you might well be familiar with this death scene. Literary critics call it a striking departure from the conventional chamber of death scene, telling us that Shakespeare himself set out to achieve something remarkable with this scene, rather like the character of the young Prince as he contemplates his position as future king.

The scene itself opens with a crowded room, full of the kings retainers or servants. This is the deathbed scene. Convention dictated that many people were present to observe the death of the king. Gory, perhaps, but in uncertain times, this was something of a requirement, just to ensure that no foulness was afoot.

The dying king calls to his servants and retainers, requesting them to leave him alone with his son, the Prince. The king curses the crown: "O polished perturbation! Golden care!". This tells use he really hasn't much enjoyed the duties of being a king. When his son enters the room, however, the king is apparently asleep. The young man, heir to the throne, mistakes the sleep for death and picks up the crown. The king then awakens to find the crown is gone. He's furious. After all, he's not dead yet! He appears to misinterpret his son's action as one of callous ambition. The king recalls his supporters and condemns the Prince before all of them in a pretty public rebuttal. The king then sends everyone else away for a second time and gives his son a serious talking-to:

Then get thee gone, and dig my grave thyself, And bid the merry bells ring to thine ear

> That thou art crowned, not that I am dead.
> Let all the tears that should bedew my hearse
> Be drops of balm to sanctify thy head.
> Only compound me with forgotten dust;
> Give that which gave thee
> life unto the worms. (110-16)

And so, the king is furious that his son appears to intend to take the crown before it is rightfully his; misinterpreting the intentions of the actions of the Prince when the crown was removed. From his torrent of rage, the king mockingly commands the Prince to go out and dig his father's grave himself. After all, that is what he appears to intend to do by "stealing" his father's crown.

Of course, the rebuttal goes on and we can only imagine how the poor Prince is feeling, having believe once that he'd lost his father; now as his father lies dying, to be firmly planted on his bad side! His father spouts out yet more venomous mockery of his son:

> *Harry the Fifth is crown'd. Up, vanity!*
> *Down, royal state! all you sage counselors, hence! And to the*
> *English court assemble now*
> *From every region, apes of idleness!*
> *Now, neighbour confines, purge you of your scum.*
> *Have you a ruffin that will swear, drink, dance,*
> *Revel the night, rob, murder, and commit*
> *The oldest sins the newest kind of ways?* (118-26)

The father implies here that his son, the royal prince, heir apparent, and – unbeknown to any of the characters – the future hero of Agincourt, will be the death and destruction of the monarchy; that he is a imp, lazy, and a criminal who will welcome barbaric practices - "rob, murder, and commit/ The oldest sins in the newest kind of ways" - when he becomes king.

Of course, poor Prince Henry was not in the least attempting to steal his father's crown and was in fact deeply moved by grief. Believing his father to be dead, the Prince was crying in the next room. After withstanding his father's censure and hearing what his father believes will be the result of his kingship, the Prince makes a winning attempt to redeem himself, reconcile to his father, and express what he actually intends for his people and his country when he becomes king.

The Prince kneels before the king, crying once again. He swears his love for his father, explaining that he was in fact full of grief when he thought him dead. He then goes on to explain his intention to regard the crown, not as a treasure, as his father believe he perceives it, but as an enemy to fight with. He intends the crown to be an entity that challenges him, that he struggles against in a sense. He intends to be a great king.

He ends his speech with an assurance that if his obligation to wear the crown becomes tainted with "any strain of pride", as his father fears, "Let God forever keep it from my head" (170-74).)

The power of a young man's intentions transform him into a new, a fundamentally different man. He goes on to conquer France, the age-old rival of England. The power of intent transforms Henry from an imp, a loose and idle man, into a resolute, just, and powerful ruler. The story at the very least confirms that it is a powerful force we are dealing with. Although the particular presentation referred to here is fictional, Henry V did indeed become a great ruler. He is remembered as one of the greatest of England's kings, no one having matched his triumphs over the French. Holding this story up as an example, then, we can begin to understand the force with which we are dealing.

As a concept, in fact, intent has received a lot of attention recently thanks to an emerging New Age philosophical movement. Digressing slightly, we may take a closer look at the Law of Attraction to see the way that intent, our intentions, are believed by many spiritual people to affect the course of our lives.

The Law of Attraction is deeply rooted in both Western and Eastern philosophies. The basic concept is communicated by the key word, "attraction". People have the power to attract and repell certain things into and out of their lives. One common expression of this is that "like attracts like".

When you want to be successful, alter your mindset to attract success into your life. Success will come provided you have estalished the right intent.

Part of the dilemma is that you probably aren't always be concious of your true intentions.

Many of us aren't aware of the way that we affect our own lives. We think we want one thing in life and we believe we're working to get it. Many of us are frustrated with our lives because we don't appear to get what we want.

The truth is, a lot of the time, we're totally wrong about what we actually want. We're also unaware of our intentions and how they manifest themselves to prevent us from getting whatever it is we mistakenly crave. To get what-you-want in life, to establish your intentions correctly, you need to practice self-awareness.

To become self-aware, you need to start to understand the type of force you're dealing with. Attraction is a power in nature. A force that affects everything in the universe one way or another so we must start of by accepting that attraction is not a force limited to interpersonal relationships.

Think for a moment about Newton's law of gravitation. Every object in the universe attracts every other object. They exert a force upon each other.

For another example of the power of attraction, look to Albert Einstein. One of his theories indicates the role of attraction in the space-time continuum. According to Einstein, all of the celestial bodies are formed due to the power of attraction. Everything in the universe from the bending of light to the motion of the stars relates to the law of attraction.

To make the most of the power of intent, the law of attraction, you need to understand the broader implications of your thoughts and feelings. They bring things into your life that are either negative or positive. depending on how you are relating to various aspects of your life.

You need to work on four elements. First, put an end to the bad habit of negativity. Stop saying things like "I can't do this" or "I won't do that". Stop using negative in your speech. Force yourself to put a positive spin on everything you say and this will put a positive spin on everything you think.

Step two involves building the power to control your intentions. You need to build up power, like you build up muscle. You can get what-you-want by expanding your fields of consciousness. One of the most profound ironies of life is that you get the material things you want in your life through spirituality.

To achieve step three, find ways of applying spirituality to every aspect of your life. *By the word "spirituality" I don't mean anything religious or theosophical. This "spirituality" has nothing to do with God, unless that is what you want it to mean. By using the word "spirituality" I mean to incorporate it deeply into your life and aspire to use this new skill and insight with an almost religious fervor.* You can begin with either your health and your relationships. Mountains of books are available on this if you need an extra boost of knowledge to be convinced.

You need to start making a "spiritual" effort every day if you want something. You need to apply the power of your intentions to achieve whatever it is you want in life.

The law of attraction, intentions, power, and spirituality are all pretty big words. They also represent big ideas.

Finally, if you want something, you need to start making a spiritual effort every day to apply your intentions, the power of your intentions, to achieve whatever it is you want.

Okay, we've talked so far about achieving things on a big scale. After all, the law of attraction, intentions, power, and spirituality are all pretty big words. They also represent big ideas. So let's start looking at intentions on a smaller scale.

Writing a book with the intent of omitting any "I" word at the beginning of the sentence may seem trivial to some but think about that for a moment. We can rely on luck to make things happen in our lives but wouldn't you rather *make* the things you want happen? The only way to do that is to intend it. As you practice making things happen your intent will only gets stronger. Thus you can see that this book is the authors exercise in intent.

Ponder this: how many of the fortuitous events of your life have come about because you ***made*** them happen? When asked this question, most people will be left with a puzzled look on their face. Others will put on the mask of victim and begin to explain how the world has put them in a bad position, with family problems, health problems, bad luck, the dog ate their homework, etc. You name it, they can give you excuse upon excuse that they willingly pass as "reasons" for their lack of success.

A sadder question to ponder (and I want you to ponder it fervently) is how many fortuitous events could you have made happen and didn't simply because you didn't choose to make them happen?

What you will find in meditating upon these questions is that your life is lacking for only one reason, **you didn't choose with intent to make things happen in your life and you replaced your intent with excuses.**

You will find that in getting what-you-want there is no greater obstacle than yourself.

The word *jihad* has entered the popular culture to mean a holy war. Within the Koran, prophet Mohammad, describes two types of jihad, the Lesser and Greater Jihad. The Lesser Jihad is the one best known and represents the holy war against an external foe.

The Greater Jihad is the one less familiar to most in the non-Islamic nations and is the battle we must wage within ourselves. The Greater Jihad demands a constant vigilance and yields an endless bounty. This book is the book of the Greater Jihad of achievement. There is no external opponent to getting what-you-want that is greater than your own internal challenges and interia. The sooner you understand this fact the sooner the world will lay down humbly at your feet.

There are some other things that you'll find in this book.

You will find the phrase "what-you-want" is used in this book as if it is a quality distinct and seperate from goals and desires. That would in fact be the case. "What-you-want" should be thought of as something powerful and distinct from everything else.

You'll find that this book is not concerned with your excuses, only your intent.

You'll find that getting what-you-want is neutral and encompasses both the best and worst of our nature.

You'll find, from the start, that this book is straightforward and direct perhaps to the point of annoyance. At the same time you'll notice some good old fashion trickery and guile.

You'll find that this book will not coddle you but encourage you and, at the same time, reject all of your BS.

You may even find this book amusing.

"Mind is the Master power that molds and makes,
And Man is Mind, and evermore he takes
The tool of Thought, and, shaping what he wills,
Brings forth a thousand joys, a thousand ills:--
He thinks in secret, and it comes to pass:
Environment is but his looking-glass."

~**James Allen**

# About The Author

There is a very strong likelihood that you will see nothing credible about the author, JK Ellis.

Aside from the fact that he's written several books on mind control and hypnosis, he claims to have used his knowledge only for good, though that claim cannot be verified.

Because he can say anything in this book he has chosen to say nothing that is favorable and good about himself.

JK Ellis has been relatively successful at maintaining his anonymity, as he refuses to give interviews and reveal the details of his life.

He enjoys pissing people off and then running away.

JK Ellis' web site is www.MindControl101.com

His blog is http://MindControl101.blogspot.com

His list of books include:

- Mind Control 101 – How to Influence The Thoughts and Actions of Others Without Them Knowing or Caring

- Perfected Mind Control – The Unauthorized Black Book of Hypnotic Mind Control

- Cult Control

# Why Is This Book Forbidden?

There are several reasons that this book takes on the ominous title of "forbidden". First of all, the word forbidden conjures up something of a magical, a supernatural significance for many. "Forbidden" is a word that stands in place of many things in life that we are tempted by, that we want. The word might almost communicate our dreams, our repressed desires, and our secret fears. Admittedly, one big reason is simple marketing. People want to have things that people tell them they shouldn't. But, that aside, there is more.

Much, much more.

You might also get the sense that the forbidden refers to control or power. Think about the messages of the major religions in the world. Almost without exception, we are told by the lofty representatives of the powers that be that the virtues of life are established in poverty, self-denial, self-sacrifice; just about every action that undermines the significance and validity of your own goals.

But what if this thinking is wrong. What if the undermining of our own significance, the significance of your own happiness, has been established as virtuous by men and women who were truly, underneath their apparent righteousness, bitter, frustrated individuals? When has self-denial truly made a person happy? What can it truly bring to an individual, let alone to others?

Let's assume we are supposed to treat others as we would like to be treated. Shouldn't they have something, some assistance that we can provide? All of that being true, if we aren't determine to get for ourselves what we want, if we don't strive to make ourselves truly happy, we can't make anyone else happy!

Okay, so what we've just said here is radical and goes against the conventional wisdom and accepted thinking. That's yet another reason that this book is forbidden. You're now beginning to get a strong sense why we call this book forbidden, right? Good. Now let's look at a couple more reasons the title of contains the word "forbidden".

While the whole purpose of this book is to change you and make you happy it will do things some people will not like.

# The Forbidden Book of Getting What You Want

This book will create great excitement and great guilt. At the same time that it dangles a delicious carrot for you to move toward it will also threaten you with a life time of misery if you don't.

To put it simply, this book is designed to manipulate you but not like a cult leader would want. This book is designed to manipulate you to do what _you_ want.

The word "manipulation" has gotten a very bad rap in recent years when in truth it is at the very core of our interpersonal and intrapersonal relationships.

### _You are supposed to be a manipulator._

You must start by not manipulating others, though that can be very fun and rewarding. You must learn to manipulate yourself. Your current success at this self-manipulation is determined by many indicators, your happiness, your satisfaction with your life, and your ability to get what-you-want. When you don't have what-you-want, if you're not satified with our life, it is safe to say you are a poor self manipulator.

By flying in the face of those people who say "Manipulation is bad." This book falls into the forbidden catagory, but there are other reasons.

## Reason #1

The first reason is that this book is about nothing loftier than getting what-you-want. This book is not about spiritual ideals, abundance thinking, manifestation consciousness, prosperity awareness, or any of the usual crap that fills the self-help shelves of a new age book store.

This book is simply about getting what-you-want.

Whether you want to get rich, get laid or get even, this is the book to read.

Please, understand this book doesn't intend to denigrate the concept of a spiritual ideal. To be a well-rounded individual one should be encouraged to develop some idea of spirituality and work to enhance it.

Remember Abraham Maslow's Hierarchy of Needs? At the bottom of the hierarchy are our survival needs; food and shelter. Once we fulfill the first level of needs we can move on to the next. Going up the hierarchy we finally reach the peak called "Self-Actualization," where we can explore the deeper parts of ourselves and our interactions with others.

What becomes clear is that when you have all your material needs met it eases the way along any spiritual path you may choose.

Now, you're going to read an even more shocking perspective. This is where you begin to make getting what-you-want a *sine qua non*[2] of your spiritual life. Elevate getting what-you-want above greed and spiritual entitlement and make it a meditative act.

By doing this you will learn the very most about yourself. You'll learn about your deeper wants and needs and about your obstacles, fears and excuses, and what it takes to overcome and to master your own inertia. By so doing you will also GET what-you-want as a side benefit to this bizare form of spiritual practice.

Who could ask for more?

## Reason #2

Another reason that this book is forbidden is that there are people in the world who are depending on your continued ignorance, desperation, poverty, and dependence to control you. They would, in no way want you to become independent and free thinking. At this point you might argue that you **are** independent and free thinking.

Are you really?

## Reason #3

One reason is because it makes getting what-you-want simple and easy and you will put consultants and would-be gurus out of business. Of course I'll admit that some people don't like taking complete responsibility for their own lives and enjoy having another person coach them to do what they already know they should do in order to be made accountable. So be it. You can spend your money anywhere you want.

Let's face it, unless you are hiring someone to teach you a new skill, most coaches and consultants do the same thing. They objectively look at your situation and your goals and tell you what you

---

2   Latin; "That without which it is nothing"

should do to most swiftly meet them. Their only asset is their objectivity and detachment.

These are assets you can build on your own with a little practice.

The thing you can do to gain this detachment is take a "big picture" approach to your goals and be flexible as you weave your way through to your ultimate ambition. For example, don't think of just the next project, sale or conquest. Think of your life as glorious campaign and each project, sale and conquest is a mere battle toward your ultimate end.

Get the picture?

When you've done this, everything begins to fit in its proper place. Decisions and choices become easier, losses are more easily coped with, victories don't go to your head and the world begins to turn in greased grooves.

Consultants and specialist will begin to hate and envy you.

## Reason #4

Another reason that this information is forbidden is that because there is nothing "nice" about how it's delivered to you. As the author of this book, being "nice" doesn't concern me. "Getting it" is important enough that if I were able to, I'd reach into your chest and rip out your heart so that you would "get it" I would. (Be glad you're on the other side of this book.)

But let's not resort to such banal demonstrations. Much better that you "get it" in a very devious and guileful fashion... A Trap.

That's right. This entire book is a trap. You may, at times, feel as if it's "high pressure" to get you to do what it takes to get what-you-want. But it's not. Everything you'll read is simply common sense. Nothing more.

By the end of this book you will have fallen for it entirely. Your only hope is to cease reading and go back to your half-lived ordinary life right NOW!

## Reason #5

One big reason this book is forbidden is that it gets right up in the face of the victim culture that permeates our society.

The victim culture insists that there are many things outside of your control. This is especially true of your emotional state that manifests itself in the sad-eyed head nodding and back-patting that accompany the words, "It's not your fault." and "You made me mad/sad/feel bad."

The entire culture insists that there are many things outside of your control and especially, that you have no control over your emotions.

The victim culture actually started with commercialism and materialism that implied that by aquiring something you don't have you will feel good. From there it degenerated into the presupposition that because happiness is external none of our feelings are within our control and that if we feel anything, bad or good, it is due to something outside of our control.

On the surface, challenging the victim culture may seem very reasonable. After all, think of all the "empowerment" workshops that are held each weekend. But even these workshops imply that control and power are external because if it weren't why would you have to go to a workshop to get it?

The victim culture enforces and encourages us to hand the rudder of our lives over to our feelings and sail ourselves into the Sargasso Sea of victim-hood.

The victim culture is based on the belief that emotions are REACTIONS to events and not CHOICES to events. As choices, we have power. As a reaction, we are puppets.

Even though this book challenges the victim culture, it does not mean that bad things don't happen to good people. Nor is it suggested that compassion, empathy and assistance shouldn't be offered. The fact is that bad things do happen to good people and compassion and assistance are ideal responses to these human tragedies. When someone is in painful need, a helping hand has more value that a lecture on how they are responcible for their own life.

The point of this book is NOT to blame people for the bad things that happen to them. The purpose is to empower people so they have more and better choices of how to respond when bad things happen.

One person I met was born of alcoholic parents and at a very early age seemed to face one obstacle after another. Many people told her "You shouldn't do that", "Don't even try." or "No one likes a show off.". Throughout her life there was a seething anger at the poor treatment given to her as she grew. Anything that posed a difficulty she could trace back to a drunken father and apathetic mother.

While blaming in this way was a familiar process and eased her mind it also made her more and more angry. She began to study the concept of personal responsibility and in a story that is much too long for this chapter she began to see things quite differently than before.

"Because I was so used to blaming my parents for my troubles at first it was hard." she said "But at the same time I realized that my blaming gave them more power than I was willing to give myself. Finally, I began to realize that I had choices and that I could not choose my parents but I did choose the best response to them at the time. Then I realized I always have choices in how I respond to things. At once I felt relieved and burdened. Relief that I have complete control over my reactions to life. Burdened by the incredible responsibility of it all. There is no way now I would go back. "

Many people have a default reaction when bad things happen and they take on the role of victim.

As defined by transactional analysis, there are two other roles that are equally debilitating that need to be examined. They are the **persecutor** and the **savior**. All of these roles limit our ability to think freely and flexibly. The Persecutor will respond with anger and contempt in the same way a Victim will respond by feeling victimized. Watch any TV drama and you'll see the characters switch back and forth from being victimized (the Victim role) to angry and vindictive (the Persecutor role). Unless you can step out of these roles, you are nothing more than a puppet. The roles you take on will manipulate you until you choose otherwise. Getting what-you-want is not likely to happen when you are under the power of these roles.

The third role is Savior, which we often take on when in the presence of someone playing either of the other roles. Think about it. For most people, being around a victim or a persecutor has little pleasure. One way to appease them is to ride in on a white horse and promise freedom from their misery or anger, i.e., playing the Savior. The problem with this is that savior is a reaction and not a choice. ALL ROLES OF THIS TYPE ARE REACTIONS, NOT CHOICES.

To get what-you-want you need more choice in how to respond to situations.

**Reason #6**

This book is forbidden because it objectifies the mass of humanity.

The philosopher, Emanuel Kant, suggested that people should not be thought of as means to an end but as ends in themselves. This book qualifies that recommendation. People are means to an end until they prove otherwise in your mind.

Doing this demands that, with regards to people, you know well your boundries and judge people by their behaviors and not their words. Only when their behaviors prove them worthy of your respect may gain your further privileges.

**Reason #7**

The basis of this book is that there is no objective reality. There is only perception. This is very disconcerting for many who ussually fear and dread any questioning to what they think is "real".

The art of getting what-you-want is done by changing your perceptions. This is not all that different from getting what-you-want from others. For it is based on the tested fact that when you control what someone percieves you control them. The distinction is that now you turn the focus onto yourself and based on your goals and desires you will focus and manipulate your perceptions manipulating yourself in the same way you would manipulate others.

Your first step can be a very humbling one, accepting as fact that your perceptions are not "real", but only choices. By making better choices of perception you create the reality you desire.

Many people would rather live in a self-made hell than question their perceptions.

### Reason #8

Another reason this book is forbidden is that by using it you will remove from others their greatest tools of manipulation: guilt and shame.

Guilt and shame have been used by the everyone from parents to organized religions to manipulate and control. Now you are stripping them of their power.

### Reason #9

You will find in this book a sacrilege that encourages a spirituality of getting what-you-want. There is no honor in poverty and self-sacrifice unless it moves you in the direction of your destiny. This book will propose that there is no greater spiritual achievement than to become a living force of nature to whom it would appear that even the gods would bow.

Of course this book is forbidden.

> *"Every man and woman is a star."*
> ~ **Aleister Crowley**

# Setting The Trap

Let's examine for a moment how most people live their lives. While everyone is capable of great things there are only a few who can say they've achieved them. These might not be achievements that the world will recognize but they should be things that, for the individual, they feel a great sense of achievement.

Sadly, very VERY few people can look back on their lives with any great sense of achievement or satisfaction. They live a life of just "getting by" as if "getting by" were good enough.

For the status quo of humanity setting the bar of achievement low is the standard. Achievement and fulfillment is the exception.

Sadly the only way to motivate most people is to not give them a choice, to put them in a trap where no matter which way they go the result will be the same.

Because we are all manipulators a carefully designed motivational trap is the highest form of human interaction. Traps of these sorts have been used and implimented by military generals, counselors, school teachers, parents and others.

The key to a successful trap is to make it not appear as a trap. Only when the sharp toothed jaws are swinging down on you do you realize what has happened. Then, of course, it's too late.

This book is designed to TRAP you into an inevitable and perhaps uncomfortable position where you will have to choose between getting what-you-want or to continue living with all the contemptible excuses for why things haven't worked out the way that you had hoped.

You're going to be trapped because, as established in the earlier chapter, most people accept the conventional wisdom that getting what-you-want, striving to achieve personal happiness through personal gain of any kind is truly selfish and thus a negative way to live your life.

Unfortunately, most people are so well indoctrinated by the conventional wisdom that they are paralyzed to do anything against it. Most people don't like to challenge the status quo. They are afraid of what they will learn about themselves and the delusions and lies that they have lived under and perpetuated in their lifetime for so long.

Your only hope to escape this trap is to put down this book and right now and walk away. Leave it for people who have ambition.

Seriously, stop for sixty seconds and just ask if you have what you really want in life.

Could you have more?

Would you want more or at least something else?

Did you answer "yes?"

Good!

The keys to power are about to be handed to you. But remember the words of Spiderman, "*With great power comes great responsibility.*" To wield that great power, you'll need to take responsibility. Something that everyone can have but few will truly accept – the responsibility for your own life and every aspect of it becomes yours with power.

So why a trap? Why would a trap be better than simply giving you instructions to follow?

The answer comes for a simple adage used in organized crime "*It's easier to motivate with a smile and a gun than with just a smile.*"

There is something deeply empowering that happens to the human psyche when one is backed against the wall and given a choice: fight or die. Many will remember the moment as horrifying but they also will attest that it is also the moment they felt most alive.

Perhaps I'm getting ahead of myself.


Let's return back to what-you-want and why you want it. Certainly what-you-want will give you something greater. What-you-want could be peace of mind, a sense of accomplishment, love, relief, satisfaction .... whatever it is, you deserve it.

Think now about the DEEPER benefit of getting what-you-want. What you'll find is that getting what-you-want can be greatly rewarding when you accept the responsibility of wielding such incredible power.... The Power of Choice.

# Getting What-You-Want Is Easy

Yes, getting what-you-want is easy because people have done it forever. You don't need metaphysical power, just an attention span and a willingness to act.

First, let's make it clear, that if you want something, there is no benefit that you'll get believing that getting it is hard.

Let's take a hypothetical example. Let's just say that you want to become the richest person in the world. Now this is a pretty hefty goal. You'd have to beat out Bill Gates and Warren Buffet with their 50 billion plus dollars. However, it can be done. First of all, you'd have to go about studying how the heck rich people become rich in the first place. Okay, many of them start out rich, but plenty of them become rich because they develop an idea, an idea that sells. They identify something that people want. Bill Gates and Warren Buffet developed Windows, an easy-to-use computer application that has been adapted and developed to serve the needs of individuals, families, small businesses, and large corporations all the world over. Now that is one heck of an idea. Other billion dollar ideas include, well, Ikea. The guy who developed Ikea furniture is currently the fourth richest man in the entire world, not all that far behind Bill Gates and Warren Buffet. How did he get rich? Well, he determined that individuals needed high quality furniture that was cheap. Let's face it, not everyone can afford to splash out tens of thousands of dollars on interior design but all of us need a comfortable bed, a table, and some chairs, maybe a couch. We all have a need for furniture in our homes, sometimes compact. Most of us, the vast majority, prefer to have nice looking stuff, good quality stuff. Why the heck shouldn't we be able to get it? Ah, well, we can, thanks to Ikea, and the owner has the money to prove how good an idea he came up with.

Yet, becoming super rich, if that's what-you-want, is not just about finding the means of getting rich.

Hypothetically, you could win the lottery tomorrow and have several million dollars in your pocket. You could invest sensibly and make several million more, and so on. Unfortunately, many people don't realize the subtlety of intent when it comes to handling money. The quality of  Intent has everything to do with everything and if you're not ready, if you're not in touch with the inner workings of your mind, you're going to fall pray to your own impulses and our own acting out of your underlying intent, the intent that you might well be unaware of.

Consider for a moment the fundamental problem of get-rich-quick-schemes. They have attained one heck of a negative reputation in the last few years, the last decade or so,

The chances are that most people take for granted the notion that getting rich is the same as being rich. Not true. This is one problem we encounter in the quest to get what we want. Many of us hold on to grose misconceptions about the actual end result we have in mind.

To be rich is one thing. Of course it means that you have a lot of money available to you. You don't have to worry about how you're going to pay your bills. You can have the things you want, whether it's good furniture, a nice house, a cool car, a great education, or a whole host of pet peeves. Who knows, maybe you want to be rich so you can buy antique jewelry! What ever it is, you've actually got to distinguish what it is that you need to do to get what-you-want.

While getting what-you-want is easy and simple you may wonder why other people haven't gotten what they want. The answer is in those words, "willingness to act".

Most people have excuses. Lots and lots of excuses. They are useful for keeping them from acting, but we can cover excuses a bit later. Most people develop their excuses in the first place when they try to get what they want and fail miserably. Why do we so often fail to get what we want? We completely misunderstand what we need! If you want to be rich – to have money, that is – you don't actually have to win the lottery. You don't have to start your own business. You don't have to get a promotion. One of the simplest things you can do is cut your overheads. Sure, it's not always possible, but before you tell yourself that it's not possible several times over, give it a try, hypothetically. What if you found a smaller house or apartment? What if you found somewhere to rent for $500 per month instead of $1000? What if you then saved the $500 for a whole year? After a whole year of saving $500 a month you'd have $6000. Okay, it's not all that much money, but say you move to a cheaper neighborhood. That means you cut back on groceries. Say you spend $400 per month instead of $600. What if you can also walk to the grocery store. You don't have to use your car as regularly. Perhaps you'd save a couple of hundred dollars on gas every month. What if you find on-street parking with your apartment. You'd be saving another $200 per month, let's say. Say that's another $500 a month you save. Now you've amassed $12,000 over the course of the year. That's a nice looking sum, right? You've also managed to achieve your goal. You have money saved. You have cut your overheads – and you don't have to deprive yourself to do that! - you're actually doing pretty well for yourself. From a good place, you can then reassess what-you-want. Do you want to make a lot of money or do you just want to have a lot of money? These two related ideas are just that. They are related ideas. They are not the same. You have to make a lot of money to live in an expensive city like New York but you don't necessary have a lot of money because you have to spend so much every month just to have the basics.

Let's pose a few questions about the statement "Getting what-you-want is easy."

- How would believing it's it's easy actually benefit you more than believe it's hard?
- Who the heck told you that getting what-you-want is hard and who are they to think that?
- Nothing about believing it's hard will make things easier; believing it's hard only makes the easy hard!
- What detailed process would someone have to go through to conclude "it's hard"?

The bottom line here is that there are a few things you'll need to understand to get what-you-want. The process is simple and easy to follow. You will realize this even more definitively when you go through the next chapter. You'll need to know the differences between goals, objectives and what-you-want. They aren't necessarily the same thing and it is often beneficial to double check that what-you-want is actually reflected in your goals and objectives; that you really understand the end result you want to achieve.

All of this will be covered next, so get ready.

# Goals, Objectives and What-You-Want

Goals, objectives and what-you-want seem as though they are the same thing but they are not. So some clearer distinctions need to be made.

There are lots of ways of thinking about what-you-want, so just start to day dream. Maybe what you want is very clear and specific as in "I want a promotion to manager of my section within the year" or it could be less specific, "I want a new car" or "I want a romantic partner" (Note the non-specific goals don't indicate the type of car or romantic partner).

Whatever you want... WRITE IT DOWN.

Do you have to WRITE IT DOWN? For the purpose of this book, YES! Writing down your goals and doing the processes are the only way you will "get it". So.... WRITE DOWN YOUR GOALS ... NOW!

As you write down your wants, hopes and desires, you clarify your goals. You goals are not "what-you-want". "What-you-want" is different from your goal.

To understand the difference between a goal and what-you-want, answer these questions in as much detail as possible

- What will having your goal give you?
- What will getting your goal allow you to feel?
- Why is getting what-you-want important to you?

You may think that these questions are asking the same thing. They are not, trust me. Collectively they help build motivation. Were these the same question just asked in a different way then the answers would *always* be the same. Let's look at each of them individually and explore their specific impact on motivation.

- **"What will having your goal give you?"**

This question will connect you directly to the benefit you get from your goal. There are a variety of benefits you can get beyond merely having attained your goal. For example, a new car may give you freedom, status, fulfill an ecological ideal or maybe you finally get an air-conditioned ride.

- **"What will getting your goal allow you to feel?"**

This question connects you more directly with the **feelings** of having your goal. This is a feeling that would propel you or compel you into action when you connect with it sufficiently. An example of this is knowing that the job you area applying for could help you make and save money and creating for you a greater sense of security. With that feeling of security you are then able to feel freedom. All because you got your job.

- **"Why is getting what-you-want important to you**?"

With this question, you get the reasons you want the goal. This is what you would say to justify going after it. You may feel the compelling feelings behind the reasons but it is the reasons we are after when we ask this question. For example, Why you want a new job may be because you want out of poverty, you want to not have to worry whenever a bill comes in the mail. That is your "why".

Asking any one of these question may be enough to create motivation. Answering all of them by writing them down with pen and paper **EVERY DAY** will build some strong (very strong) motivation. Keep adding to the list if you're not motivated enough by continueing to ask and answer the questions. Keep adding to your list of motivating answers until the motivation increases.

One of the best known techniques for goal setting and management is refered to as SMART. We're going to encounter this again a bit later. The reason why we'll cover it twice in this book is because it's so darned important! We will also use it here to illustrate a piont.

SMART is used by many of the world's top organizations to assess the nature of goals. Many of the most successful individuals in the world also use this goal setting technique to achieve whatever it is they want.

According to the SMART programs, your goals should be all of the following:

**Specific** – Ask yourself if you clearly defined your goal?
**Measurable** – Ask yourself if you know that you are making progress?
**Achievable** – Ask yourself if your goal really achievable? Be honest.
**Rewarding** – Ask yourself if your your goal something you are willing to make sacrifices for?
**Timely** – Ask yourself if your goal is achievable in a meaningful time frame?

If you can be fairly sure that your goals are SMART, you can set about achieving them. How do you start to achieve? Many life coaching experts recommend setting a twenty-five year plan of smaller goals to complete one by one. Add these twenty-five small goals up and the sum total should be the realization of your lifetime plan.

Having set a twenty-five year plan, you should then set a five year plan. After that, set a one year plan, a six month plan, and a one month plan. Attack your life goals in small chunks and you are far more likely to achieve them than if you tackle the entire sum total of everything you want to achieve in one go.

Establish progressively smaller goals to meet your lifetime goals and base each set on the previous plan. Try to set a daily to-do list of things so that you can keep focused on achieving. We'll talk about excuses later but the general idea of goal setting is to put a stopper in your own mouth so you don't go off spouting those excuses to yourself.

The steps you take during the first days, the first months may be very simple. You may just want to just gather information in preparation for more active pursuit of you goals. You may just want to read certain books that will help toward the achievement of your goals in the long run. Whatever it is, in the beginning you should work to improve the quality and realism of your goal setting. Do whatever it takes to make sure you are on the right track. Stay on track by regularly reviewing your plans, and making sure that they continue to fit the way you want to live your life.

Make a habit of reviewing and updating your to-do list, your daily to-do list, and your longer-term list. Review and update your daily goals on a daily basis if possible. Longer term plans you can periodically review and modify to reflect any changes in priorities or experience.

Keep this process in mind:

1. Write each goal as a positive statement.

2. Be precise by establishing dates, times, and amounts so that you can measure your achievement.

3. Set priorities for each goal to avoid becoming overwhelmed. This will also direct your attention to the most important goals.

4. Write goals down regularly and repeatedly as this helps you keep them focused.

5. Keep low-level goals you work to on a daily basis small and achievable as keeping goals small and incremental gives you more opportunities to reward yourself.

6. Take care to set goals over which you have as much control as possible. The best approach is to keep your goals focused on personal performance.

7. It is important to set goals that you can achieve, in full recognitions of your own desires and ambitions.

8. Do not set goals too low but establish goals just slightly out of your immediate grasp.

Be sure that you enjoy achieving your goals, short-term, and long-term. Absorb the implications of the goal achievement. Monitor and revel in your progress towards your life goals. Reward yourself and make sure you're enjoying the journey.

Another important step is to keep reviewing your goals. Check the following:

- Have you been achieving your goals too easily? Make your next goals harder achieve.

- Are your goals taking too long to achieve? Make your next set of goals a little easier to achieve.

- Have you learned something that might lead you to change other goals? Change the relevant goals.

- Have you noticed a deficit in your skills? Set new goals to resolve this.

Failure to meet goals does not matter. What matters is the positive and measurable actions you take toward those goals because if you know the steps to take and take them the goals will be achieved.. Should some action you take not work then modify it or do something different.

Think of Thomas Edison who proclaimed to have learned a thousand different ways how ***not*** to make a light bulb before he found out one that worked. He just kept doing something different until he got what he wanted.

Learn from your failures and your mistakes. Failure does not have to be a negative thing. Learning lessons, incorporate them into your goal-setting program. Your goals may very well change as you mature. Adjust your goals to reflect growth in your personality. You may find that some of your goals are no longer attractive to you, let them go and let go of any emotions associated with them.

Goal setting should bring you real pleasure, satisfaction and a sense of achievement. The next chapters include a few other points about "what-you-want" and "objectives" to consider. Look at them one by one to help determine the best course of action for your work.

"Look at every path closely and deliberately, then ask ourselves this crucial question: Does this path have a heart? If it does, then the path is good. If it doesn't, it is of no use."

~ **Carlos Castenada**

# What-You-Want

Let's make it clear, what-you-want is not the same thing as your goal.

What-you-want is what you will get when you have your goal.

Think about it, you may want a car for all sorts of reasons, but having that car will give you something greater. That could be a sense of pride, status, peace of mind or a sense of power. What you will notice is that what-you-want will express itself far beyond your car. What-you-want will let that "something bigger" begin to permeate other aspects of your life and IT FEELS GOOD.

Take a moment to imagine yourself having acquired your goal. Maybe it's a job promotion. Maybe it's a new car. Put yourself there in that moment and see what you would see, hearing what you would hear and feeling what you would feel. Make the images big and bright. Now lock that feeling into place.

*That feeling* is what-you-want.

Think about it. Let's suppose your goal is a new car. When you accomplish a goal and get your new car you get that feeling. You get what-you-want. With that feeling of what-you-want in your life other things in your life begin to change and improve. You begin to notice that pride, status, peace-of-mind, and sense of power even during other times away from your car. When you get what-you-want, you start to be in better mood, you begin to treat people differently (better, I hope), you anger less and deal with stress in creative and resourceful ways.

The point of the distinction between goals and what-you-want is that goals are the best most logical avenue to getting what-you-want.

When you connect with the understanding that you are truly going after something bigger than a goal, then your goals become more focused and your motivation becomes stronger. Getting what-you-want will be your compass. Your goals will be your map.

To create motivation many people demand an enemy to face to make them ready for the effort. For you the enemy is everpresent. The enemy is your own complacency, inertia and indifference.

By following the processes in this book you can pull yourself from the complacent and indifferent feelings and create both a feeling of passion to go after your desires and pain and regret for any action or inaction that slows your progress.

The next step is to use that motivation to create a plan toward the achievement of your goals and getting what-you-want. That plan will be composed of a series of smaller steps called objectives.

# Objectives

One way of thinking about objectives is to consider them as a subset of goals. All objectives are goals but not all goals are objectives.

---

**Foreshadowing:** In a few short chapters you'll learn the **secret** to getting what-you-want in a way that is easy and simple. The part that you're about to read now is an essential step to understanding the remainder of this book, so pay attention.

---

An objective is a goal that meets five criteria. You can remember this by using the acronym S.M.A.R.T., which stands for **S**pecific, **M**easurable, **A**ttainable, **R**ealistic and **T**ime bound.

Let's look at these criteria in more detail.

The first two letter of S.M.A.R.T. stand for **S**pecific and **M**easurable. Why is specific and measurable important? The short answer is so that you can know when you've achieved your outcome.

Many people set a goal to "lose weight" and don't get anymore specific than that. Because there is nothing specific or measurable about "lose weight," they could achieve their goal with a simple bowel movement. When they have one, you can tell them, "Congratulations!"

But because their goal was not specific and measurable, they would then explain, "that is not what I meant".

Of course. What can they expect if they're not specific?

Perhaps you heard of the ancient story of the magical genie who would bestow three wishes to anyone who released him from the bottle that imprisoned him. The catch was that the genie never asked them to be specific about their wishes and attaining each wish would inevitably make them worse than before they asked.

The lucky person would tell the genie "My wish is to have a million dollars." By granting the wish the genie bestows a million single dollar bills in the back seat of the lucky persons car. He is first assailed by people wanting to rob him only to later be audited by the Internal Revenue Service.

The genie's benefactor then asks for his problem to go away and he is returned back to a state of poverty.

Realizing that he now has only one wish remaining he humbly asks for a long life with great power and respect. The genie promptly turns the man into a fellow genie and traps him in a bottle.

The moral of this story is to be very VERY specific about your goal and be able to break your goal down into very specific outcomes. Were you to lack specificity in your goal you may run the risk of getting exactly what you asked for.

Another example is from the TV show, "The Twilight Zone".

A man asks the Devil to make him the absolute ruler of a country. The Devil grants his wish by making him Adolph Hitler on the day he commits suicide in the bunker. An aide hands him the gun with which he will shoot himself as the sounds of Allied artillery boom all around him.

Do you think it might have helped if the man had been more specific about what kind of rulerr he wanted be, in what kind of country and in what circumstances?

Not being specific about your goals and objectives will probably not have such dire consequences for you, but I hope you can see the value of being more specific than you have been in the past.

The next two letters are **A** and **R** ,which stand for "**A**ttainable" and "**R**ealistic". Ask yourself if the objective is realistic for you to attain. A"no" answer means you need to reevaluate the objective and modify it to something that is attainable and realistic.

For example, if you want to buy a red 1965 Corvette convertible (note that this is measurable and specific) but your current financial resources prevent you from accomplishing that, then you can still hold the goal of a red 1965 Corvette convertible but your objectives can be focused on ways of improving your income. This step will encourage you to think in smaller more realistic terms while holding on to the big picture of your goals.

As an example, Bob wanted to create his own profitable Internet business but he realized that he knew nothing more about Internet business than turning on his computer and buying things on Ebay. From that onset Bobs goal might have seemed overwhelming.

To accomplish his goal Bob started making Attainable and Realistic goals. He then listed all the things he had to learn which included how to design web pages, how to write sales copy, setting up autoresponders, fulfillment centers and more.

He worked it out in as much detail as possible to determine if each step was attainable and realistic. As the details became clear he determined that he could achieve each goal and as a result create his Internet business.

The final letter in the S.M.A.R.T. acronym is **T** for "Time bound," meaning the objective is part of a time line with a deadline for accomplishment.

This deadline too must be attainable and realistic.

Having a deadline for an outcome is important and it makes the outcome something that is definitely within your control. When you realize that ALL the aspects of the goal are under your control (if you did the process correctly), then attaining your goal is a simple matter of doing a series of S.M.A.R.T. outcomes. A deadline can create excitement because when it's all laid out, each outcome you achieve simply affirms the certainty of attaining your ultimate goal.

There is one circumstance when a deadline is not needed. That is when the outcome is about **how** you are going to do something. Another way of thinking about this is when you want to develop a certain style of living. This will be an outcome that that has no end.

A good example of this would be if you had lived your early years in poverty and abuse. Your objective (without a deadline) would then be to live un-oppressed and financially comfortable. While this is an ongoing way of living and does not contain a deadline it must be attainable and realistic.

This is often thought of as a form of mission statement, which would include all the characteristics you wish to demonstrate as you live your life and achieve your goals. More on this later.

S.M.A.R.T. objectives are all very attainable only because they meet S.M.A.R.T. Criteria. As an example of using the S.M.A.R.T. criteria, I was once talking with a young friend who was within a year from graduating high school. He shared with me his secret ambition of becoming a naval fighter pilot. The conversation began with my asking him that if he was already a naval fighter pilot, what did he do just prior to becoming one?

The answer was going to pilot training.

Then I asked what would have to happen prior to that. The series of questions continued in the same vein as we worked backwards in time to the present. We made sure each answer fit the S.M.A.R.T. criteria until we reached his present moment in time and we wrote down every step. After reviewing the timeline that we created he felt as if his future was predestined and all he had to do if follow the map that he had laid out. His confidence seemed to skyrocket from that 20 minute conversation.

This could be you when you use the S.M.A.R.T. criteria.

You might ask me if my young friend ever attained his goal of becoming a naval pilot. The truth is I never found out. That was in his hands and not mine.

Keep reading and you'll learn how to turn the confidence you will gain from S.M.A.R.T. goals into an everyday experience.

---

"The man who is intent on making the most of his opportunities is too busy to bother about luck."

**~ B. C. Forbes**
(Scottish born American Editor and Founder of Forbes Magazine (1917). 1880-1954)

---

# Goals vs. Intent

The word "Intent," with a capital "I," is going to take on a magical property. One of the first things to note is that we are considering a goal to be something different from an Intent. Anyone can set goals. The question is, do they follow them up with intent? Do they intend to achieve those goals? Let's begin be distinguishing between a goal and an intent.

One way to distinguish between a goal and an intent is to think of a goal as an "I want..." and an intent as "I will..." but it's an "I will" that includes a very detailed understanding of what needs to happen. An Intent includes every S.M.A.R.T. outcome and where they lay upon the time line. An Intent, when it becomes magical, makes getting what-you-want a *fait accompli.*

We are, however, going to dwell a little longer on the concept of intent before we move on. First of all, your intentions must be alligned with your goals. Be warned, if you do not allign these two elements in your planning and in your actions, without doubt you will lose out on achieving your goals. We mentioned briefly the problem that many people have when it comes to goals and intentions. Most people incorrectly identify what it is that they want in life. They incorrectly assume that they know what they want. They try to pursue whatever it is they think they want but their subconscious mind does not allow them to succeed in the quest. Ultimately, our unconscious minds are more sensitive to what we want than our conscious minds. Consciously we might believe that a lot of money, women, and popularity will make us happy. Subconsciously we might consider that only being debt free, having a satisfying job, maintaining a stable relationship, and living close to a few good friends is what will really work at keeping us happy and healthy in life.

Look at any number of celebrities. Britney Spears and Lindsey Lohan provide great examples of truly unhappy people. Let's face it, anyone who goes to the extremes of shaving their heads, runs through several relationships, has children with a man of questionable character, and apparently spends a substantial portion of money on drugs and booze, well, anyone who knows anything about pop psychology will tell you that the person is deeply unhappy. Yet both Spears and Lohan, even the likes of Michael Jackson, Billie Joel, Clark Gable and Paris Hilton all have or had considerable wealth, they are incredibly popular – presumably some of the most popular and well known individuals in the United States, if not the world – and they have access to virtually anything and everything. Still, they're not happy. Should we condemn celebrities and the wealth for this? Are they selfish to be thinking and behaving this way? On the one hand, sure, probably they are. On the other hand, well, no they're not. Self-destructive behavior displayed by celebrities often has a lot to do with underlying unhappiness. The unhappiness steams from the fact that most celebrities trade themselves, their privacy and many other elements of who they are in exchange for fame and fortune. Fame and fortune are not what they actually want and so they act out.

Now consider what it would be like to have both an Intent to achieve a goal and an Intent to live a certain life-style. What if you actually determined what it is you want in life and what you need to achieve those things? What you will have done is an intentionally designed a life, a very full and rich life, in which achieving the various goals are almost inevitable.

Why?

Because everything fits, from what you want to accomplish to how you're going to achieve these things. You will even have planned out how you'll deal with your successes and failures. This comes not from achieving the goals but from the journey of achieving them.

One of the best historical examples of someone who has lived this ideal is Benjamin Franklin (1707 – 1790), who helped found the United States of America. He was a statesman, an inventor, and an entrepreneur.

Early on, in the midst of his youthful ambition to achieve his various goals in life, he set out to live by a high standard. He created a list of 13 "virtues" that he vowed to live by. Temperance, Order, Resolution, Frugality, Moderation, Industry, Cleanliness, Tranquility, Silence, Sincerity, Justice, Chastity and Humility were the virtues to which he aspired. On a daily basis he would look at his list of virtues and evaluate how well he had lived up to these ideals. At the same time, he would evaluate how his ambitions could best fulfill those virtues. Needless to say, his life was FULL of accomplishments and he never felt as if he was finished.

Every part of his life was refined to a fine edge and he viewed every action he took as a step to further sharpen that edge.

On a scale of one to ten, the importance what you've just read ranks as a 15+. **Don't be an idiot with this information.** Read it again to get the impact.

## Recap of the Main Points

Okay let's look at what you've learned.

- You've learned there is a distinction between a goal, an outcome and what-you-want.

- You've learned that the fulfillment of a goal gives you something greater... what-you-want.

- You've learned that an objective is a type of goal that is Specific, Measurable, Attainable, Realistic and Time bound i.e, S.M.A.R.T.

- You've learned that by listing all the S.M.A.R.T. objectives that make up your goal and doing them you will attain your goal and ultimately get what-you-want.

- You've learned that you can also create goals and objectives about _**how**_ you wish to live your life. Because these goals are ongoing and persistent there is no need for deadlines.

- You've learned that when you choose to live this way you can accomplish more than anyone has ever thought possible.

The purpose of this book and the following exercises is to help you develop a second sight. This second vision will be clearly forcused on the future while you involve yourself in the everyday activities of the here and now.

Your second sight will be the rudder that steers you through the politics of everyday life and lands you at your goals.

## An Exercise in Intent

There is a very simple exercise to strengthen your intent. What you do is pick an act that you intend to do and ***do it.***

It doesn't matter whether you are constructing a building or baking a cake. To do either one of them, you must intend to do it. For some this "doing it" could be a huge effort and others it may find it tedious. Regardless, the act had to be intended.

Therefore pick some action, any action, and intend to do, and then ***do it!*** Because it's the fulfillment of the intent that matters. Do it whether the action is practical or arbitrary. Your intent could be to deposit your paycheck or jump on one foot for twenty seconds.

Do it!

---

"Intent is not a thought, or an object, or a wish. Intent is what can make a man succeed when his thoughts tell him that he is defeated. It operates in spite of the warrior's indulgence. Intent is what makes him invulnerable. Intent is what sends a shaman through a wall, through space, to infinity."

~ **Carlos Castaneda**

---

# Becoming a Force of Nature

There are people who live their lives as if they were a force of nature. They seem to always get what they desire and be unaffected by the events around them. Around these people others make it a rule to follow them or get out of their way. These "forces of nature" can be violent and demanding or seductive and compelling, or both. They often personify an energy. This energy may be specific or undefined in nature.

An example is the fictional Darth Vader who personifies an energy of sheer will.

A living example of this type of persona is Playboy magazine founder, Hugh Hefner, who is the personification of the power of hedonistic fulfillment and Eros.

Napoleon Bonaparte, Salvador Dali , Gambino crime boss John Gotti and former president Bill Clinton are others to name a few. Not all of these "forces of nature" seek fame. Many aspire only to live their lives as they wish.

Have you ever met someone who lives life as if they are force of nature?

When you've taken the opportunity to speak with them, what you'll learn is that they can tell you *exactly* what they are going to accomplish. They will tell you this with a calm and unshakable sense of certainty. They may even seem as if they have already accomplished it or as if they have seen the future and have come back to tell you what will happen.

Because they have thought so thoroughly about what they want and how they want to live as they go after it, unforeseen events are rare and of little consequence.

The worst thing an unforeseen event might do is delay the inevitable attainment of their goal.

When the unforeseen occurs they have a plan on how they will respond. That is the depth of their self-understanding.

Anyone who is within the presence of these rare people will feel both a soothing calmness and an unstoppable force emanating from their character.

Upon first evaluation, one might conclude that these living monoliths of achievement are motivated by endless ambition but that would be inaccurate. Rather, they are moved by an unshakable sense of destiny.

While these people appear human in every way, they seem to move through the world more like a force of nature in and of themselves. Life is an adventure and their goals and accomplishments are landmarks and milestones of their journey. They view success and failure with an unwavering detachment. Their intent is so firm that all they know is their goal *will* be accomplished. Time is of no consequence to them because, like a god looking down from Mount Olympus, eventually all will transpire as they have laid it out and neither the winds, the waters nor the wills of man can stop them.

They make their achievements seem easy and cause us to ask, "Why shouldn't I be able to do what they do?"

This is the life YOU could live, all you must do is choose it.

## Your Outward Appearance

This section is not about dressing for success because even an idiot can do that. This is about your presentation as a person and how you move and interact with those around you.

The first advice is simple: *Move as if you have a purpose.* Moving as if you have a purpose means moving as if you are not just pulled though space but also through time. You are being pulled in the direction of your goals.

This is important for two reasons. The first is you *do* have a purpose and even though you may never discuss it outwardly it is through your purposeful actions and movements that others will take note and either assist you or move out of your way.

The second reason is more subtle and internal. When you move as if you have a purpose you are intentionally affecting your physiology. Any actor trained in "method acting" will tell you that if you do enough outward expressions of an emotional state you will begin to *feel* that emotional state take hold of you.

Moving with a purpose will strengthen every aspect of your purpose.

During the early part of the last century a young reporter was instructed to visit Mohandas Ghandi at a hospice for the dying in India and ask to observe Ghandi as he went about his daily routine. What he observed seemed unappearant at first but quickly became obvious. Ghandi moved as if he was being *pulled* by some greater force. That force was his sense of purpose.

## Create a Mythology

One way to strengthen your sense of purpose is to create a mythology that describes your life and then live to fulfill it.

Many people have created their personal mythology from thin air and have often been revealed as frauds. To avoid this remember that almost every good hero of mythical greatness begins with a humble origins. This holds true in the stories from the biblical Moses to the fictional Luke Skywalker. Start your mythology where you are at and build on it. By asking yourself 'What would the very best me do?' you can direct your course with acts that seem as though you are pulled in the direction of your greater purpose.

## Your Internal State Of Mind

There is a constant force that is created when we have a goal and make a plan to go after it. The force is that not everything will go our way, the difference between what we plan and what actually occurs. This is often refered to as "Friction". This Friction is a constant componant of life; we plan one thing grandiose and some unforseen event stalls our progress.

Friction is not an enemy but a natural element which, like the weather, we can sometimes predict, but seldom control. Fighting the friction of life is as futile as fighting a huricane so instead let it become your teacher as you become it's most dutiful student.

What it teaches is the endless value of flexibility and being able to adapt to changing situations. There will always be friction therefore there will always be lessons to learn.

Friction cannot be pleaded with or manipulated. Friction is as cold and uncaring as the winter sea but it can be a teacher as wise as Aristotle.

To become a Force of Nature you must abandon whatever doubt you have whether or not we each deserve to have what we deeply want. What is proposed is that you should get what-you-want *if* you know in precise detail what you want, and *if* you know in precise detail the steps to getting it, and *if* you are absolutely willing to do each step, and *if* you are flexible enough to embrace and adapt to the friction of life.

---

"This is the true joy in life - being used for a purpose recognized by yourself as a mighty one; being thoroughly worn out before you are thrown on the scrap heap; being a force of nature instead of a feverish selfish little clod of ailments and grievances."

~George Bernard Shaw
British playwright & novelist
(1856 – 1950)

---

# The Trap is Set

You now know everything you need to accomplish your goals and get what-you-want

You know that what-you-want is bigger than any goal and is the sole motivation in life to do and accomplish anything.

You know that choosing a lifestyle helps you define how you are going to live and accomplish your goals.

You know that ultimately you and you alone are completely responsible for your feelings. No one but you can make you mad, sad or frustrated.

You know that you alone are responsible for your life from this point forward.

You even know what to do to accomplish your goals, live your ideal lifestyle and become a force of nature.

You know it and you know you know it.

Earlier I mentioned I would trap you. Here is the trap: Now that you know what you know, you can either choose to live a better life and get what-you-want or you can choose to just live the way you always have. The choice is yours and it's completely under YOUR control.

---

**Intent**

My Intent is Unbending.
My Focus Unending.
Every piece is a part of the whole.
Every thought that I think...
Every movement I make...
Every action I take...
Brings me closer and closer to my goal.

~**Darlo Okasi**

---

# The Choice

You have a choice, a simple choice.

You have the choice now between going after your goals and getting what-you-want or making excuses. There is no third option. That is the choice. There are no other options.

If you choose to go after your goals, you are going to learn a considerable amount about your true self. For some people – for most of us, in fact – this is a very daunting prospect. Truthfully, however, it is important to get in touch with who you are at some point in your life.

Of course, you're also going to experience a lot of change. Although no one in this world is a stranger to change, many people are still afraid of it and look to avoid it as much as possible. Yet change effects us daily whether we go looking for it or not. Change can consume our daily lives if we don't approach the problem properly.

Before you go ahead and make your choice, one way or another, take note of the best ways to go about accepting change. First of all, accept that everything, both good and bad, change. Look hard enough and you will find something useful, good, and healthful in the new situation. Second of all, you should try to participate in the changes that occur in your life, in your personal life, in your professional life, and in the broader sense, in the life of your community. You should not react to change out of necessity but you should try to find better ways to embrace it. Take control and don't let other people or events dictate the outcome of your life. Finally, you should also try to recognize that your actions, your Intent, influences the outcome of situations.

The bottom line, as state above, is that you have a simple but very significant choice to make.

This may seem like a high pressure tactic, to make it this simple but it's not. That is just the way it is. Think about it. You will either go after what-you-want or find some excuse not to.

Any excuse is as good as another. Pick one: you're too busy. Your family won't support you. You're not patient enough. The dog ate your homework. One excuse is as good as any other.

Now that you know it's all your choice is there really much of a choice?

Which will you choose to do, get what-you-want or make an excuse? The life of excuses will have much the same to offer as now. Very likely, your life will not be that much different than how it was before. You'll have the very same pleasure and the very same disappointments.

But what would it be like if you chose a life that was different than your current life... or any one else's? The choice is to decide if your life will be determined by people and events or by your own Intent.

What would it take to make that choice?

What would you have to do?

What would you have to give up?

The very first things you would have abandon are your excuses.

This may seem like a very high pressure tactic but it's not. The whole concept is quite logical. Think about it. You will either go after what-you-want or find some excuse to not do it. Excuses all help you accomplish the same result which is staying where you are at.

Even if you agree to not do anything, you're agreeing to live with your excuses.

Should you choose the life of excuses then life is likely to not be that much different than how it was before.

Choose to go after what-you-want and nothing will ever be the same.

---

Nothing is impossible; there are ways that lead to everything, and if we had sufficient will we should always have sufficient means. It is often merely for an excuse that we say things are impossible.

~**Francois De La Rochefoucauld**

# Excuses

Let's look at excuses. There are bad excuses and good excuses. For an excuse to be good it has to apply to everyone who has been in the same situation without exception. A person might say "I can't enter a marathon because I lost my right leg in a car accident." Were that a truly good excuse there would not be an amputee class in marathon events. What you'll find is that there are many excuses but very few good excuses.

Most people only need one excuse to stop them from going any further. Other people need more than one excuse to stop them. Consider that some people, in fact many of us, have a threshold limit of excuses. This means that one single external event would not stop some people but if there were two or three or more they reach their threshold, saying that it's just too much for them.

When you reach the threshold of X number of excuses then that becomes the excuse. You can hear it often when someone gives a litany of reasons why they didn't accomplish things. But the bottom line is; Their intention was just not firm enough.

Let's take a diversion and for a moment talk about Mahatma Gandhi. Anyone who has studied twentieth century history will likely agree it was through his unbending intent and persistent efforts that India was able to break free from colonial England. He had an unending list of excuses why he should **not** succeed. He was just one man against a great military empire. India was divided politically and religiously. England had a limitless ability to enforce the rule of law through aggression was evident.

Yet somehow this skinny, poor man led the impoverished nation of India to rebel in such a unique and non-violent way that England had to agree that the colonization of india was no longer worth their time. As a result, they handed governmental control over to India in 1947, after over ninety years of iron handed colonial rule.

To Gandhi, excuses did not matter. No matter how many setbacks he experienced, no matter how impossible it seemed to others, no matter how discouraged others felt, Gandhi held firm to his Intent.

The point is that Gandhi had no threshold limit of excuses. His intent was firm. He would not waver and he **_knew_** he would see his goal of an independent India, regardless of how long it took.

How easy would it be for you to get what-you-want if you had Gandhi's strength of Intent?

But let's look at some really good excuses one at a time and just see how good they a really are.

### "There is no money."

Yeah. Gandhi didn't have money. The truth is that very few people start out in life with money. Yet so many of them are able to accomplish things and get what they want by their genius. Their financial assets may be limited but not their creative assets. To think that without money you should give up on your goals is foolish. You're simply focusing on money and not on creativity.

Neuro Linguistic Programming (NLP) has a precept that is good to live by. "When something doesn't work, then do something different." This makes incredible sense yet there is no end of people who discover that if what they are doing isn't giving them the results they want they just do it more and harder.

Don't be an idiot. Set your intent, assess your situation, make a plan and work it. Should any unforeseen events delay your goal then reevaluate your plan, make a change and continue on.

### "There is not enough time."

Like any goal and any desire to get what-you-want, you are going to have to evaluate/reevaluate your life and determine what is realistic and attainable (remember the S.M.A.R.T. objectives).

Time is certainly a factor to consider. When your time is filled, you simply have to reevaluate the deadlines you set for yourself and, at the same time, strengthen your intent..

Suppose you dreamed of being a doctor but a family crisis prevented you from going to medical school right out of college. All that **_truly_** did was push the deadline back. Nothing more.

Hold on to your intent. Know why it's important to you and be unmoved by the "slings and arrows of outrageous fortune."

## "There is too much work involved."

Believe me, I understand because I'm lazy too. There is a solution that comes from spending a lot of time creating a detailed plan filled with a timeline of S.M.A.R.T objectives. When you have that detailed plan you don't have to think much about what to do next because **it's written in the plan**.

Having a plan that you can work will help you accomplish your goals and maintain a "lazy" life style. Consider the **power** you would have to honestly admit how lazy you are and still be able to accomplish your goals.

The truth is you won't be lazy. You'll simply be doing things that you know you can easily do and you'll be doing them in a very sequential order. The whole process will seem easy and support the "laziness" that resides within you.

Some of the people I've worked have had the experience of going through military special forces training and repeated the phrase to me "The more you sweat in training the less you bleed in combat." which is their way of saying "Do your planning and work your plan." Planning and working your plan, you will find, is the lazy persons way to getting what-you-want.

## "My health is not good."

There are two things you can do that will help if you are physically challenged at accomplishing your goal. The first is to build your resources of people, friends, employees, etc., that you can delegate things to. Your so-called limitations can be the best friends to your creativity.

The second thing that you can do is consider improving your health as a goal. Granted, there are people out there with very serious and challenging health problems but there is usually something about that situation that is under their control. A paraplegic can still go to the gym. A diabetic can more seriously monitor blood sugar, diet and exercise to optimize their heath. A cancer sufferer can be determined to do everything to conquer their illness

Health should be part of what-you-want anyway.


## "I'm too old to do this."

Let's look at this one realistically with a one-word answer: Bullshit!!

What does age have to do with ANYTHING when 12-year-olds can start a business and 80-year-olds run marathons, swim the English channel and get their first diploma?

There is no upper or lower age limit for getting what-you-want.


## "I had a bad childhood."

Let's consider the excuse that many people use: the past.

People often use the past to justify their fears, compulsions, depression and any number of reasons they don't go after what they want.

Through their past experience they were taught that these responses were useful and, at that time, they were. Through learning to fear they protected themselves from an alcoholic parent or from some form of humiliation. They found relief through eating and they developed a compulsion to eat, gamble or use drugs. All of this offered relief *at that time.* As a result these fears and compulsions became deeply ingrained and a habit developed that leaves the person paralyzed to act effectively. The point is that while those behaviors worked then, they no longer are of use.

And it's all blamed on the past.

Most therapists deal with these fears and addictions with compassion and understanding but for the sake of getting what-you-want **the past does not matter.**

Yes, it seems heartless and devoid of compassion to say it. Still it's true. **The past does not matter** when it comes to getting what-you-want. What matters is only what you do now and from this point forward.

What-you-want is a reason to live fearlessly and surpass your limitations.

To free yourself from the clutches of the past make what is happening in your present and future urgent, as if your very life depended on what you are doing **right now.**

You'll find that the weighty burden of the past is easy to let go of when a gun of urgency is staring you in the face. The past can be used as a foundation on which to build or an anchor to hold you back.

The choice is yours.

**"The dog ate my homework."**

This one I had to throw in because it makes all excuses begin to look very , very silly.

If you want it, then it's reason enough to go after it.
Empires are not built on excuses.

Ships do not sail because of excuses.

Movies are not produced on excuses.

# Life isn't measured by the quality of your excuses!

There is an understanding that is drilled into every cadet at West Point military academy. When asked a question there are only four acceptable answers: "Yes, sir." "No, sir." "No excuse sir." and "I don't understand."

The essence of this chapter is about responsibility and especially being responsible for your life.  This  isn't about blame or shame or guilt. All those emotions were built in during the past and there is nothing you can do about them now.

Yet, from this moment onward you can take charge of your present and your future actions and live intentionally – without excuses.

> "A man of knowledge lives by acting, not by thinking about acting."
>
> ~ Carlos Castaneda

# Making It Easier
### (by making it all fit together)

Let's lay this all out in some simple form that recaps what you've already read.

**Step 1**
**Determine what you really want.**

The goal may be the thing or achievement you are going after. That will give you a feeling. The feeling is "what-you-want" because it will motivate you to take the steps needed to accomplish your goal.

An important roadmap or blueprint to establish in addition to a business plan is certainly one that outlines a plan to achieve personal development. A simple list or a series of statements about what you want can serve as a plan. Regardless of how you decide to lay out your plan, you should look to establish goals in the following areas to enjoy a complete life:

1. *Your Personal Life* – you can be single, in a relationship, or married (or somewhere in between). Whatever your feelings about love and relationships, determine what you want for your personal life. Love and a sense of self-love through intimate relationships will help you create the strength you need to go to work.

2. *Your Relationships* – like it or not, your family is the strongest link you have to the past. You are welcome to define "family" in any way that suits you. Family could have a traditional meaning of parents, grand parents and children or your "family" could mean your closest friends and associates. Family is about the relationships you build and develop that matters. Whatever effort you make, it will count towards something. Work to reinforce a positive relationship with your family.

3. *Your Career* – we often get side tracked when it comes to our career goals no matter how closely we followed the advice of our guidance counselors. Try to rectify this in your own life. Maybe there is some

aspect of your professional life that you haven't addressed in a while, factor this into your plan for personal development.

4. *Your Intellectual Development* – knowledge is food for the mind just as spirituality is good for the soul. You can join your local library and commit to read one book a month just to build your intellect. You could start playing a mental game like bridge or chess. Exercising the mind improves memory and helps to prevent the onset of diseases such as Alzheimer's that cause the degeneration of the brain. Treat your mind like a muscle. Exercise it regularly; keep it in shape. A strong mind is an excellent asset to have whatever your goals.

5. *Your Spiritual Development* – you don't have to be religious to be spiritual. Spirituality is about getting in touch with the world at large and with deeper parts of yourself. One way of thinking about spirituality is to ask if there is any belief or quality that you want to be in every part of your life. By working to apply that quality or belief in such an in depth way you focus your attentions and allow it to affect every part of your life. Thus this does not have to be a religious belief or even one that included a belief in God. What is does include is **something** that is deeply important to you that you wish to have in every aspect of your life.

6. *Terms of Your Physical Well-Being* – you should work to develop your body as many people have a lot of baggage associated with their appearance. We're all subject to the media cult. We're all supposed to look like a billion dollars. To improving your physical well-being does not mean you should starve yourself or push yourself to your physical limits. Healthy physical well-being involves eating a balanced diet with the right amount of calories, vitamins, minerals, and fiber. The right amount of exercise is what you feel comfortable with. At least three half-hour work outs per week are recommended for the average, healthy adult. Examine how you live at present. Are you eating enough fruit and vegetables per day? Are you drinking enough water? Moderate exercise is a great way to reduce stress. You will produce the natural stress reducing hormones of endorphins. You'll almost

certainly feel more relaxed and focused as you start integrating a physical regime and good eating habits into your routine.

All of these elements should help you move along the road to getting what-you-want.

As an example, being a better golfer may be your goal. You may have gotten specific by setting your goal to lower your handicap by two strokes. But this is just your goal. You've even asked what would being a better golfer with a lower handicap give you and found your what-you-want. The answer is it give you a feeling of pride and accomplishment and a greater feeling of self confidence.

So your goal will be the missile that delivers the what-you-want payload.

Thus if you know you are acting in ways that will improve your golf game you know that the feeling of pride , accomplishment and self confidence are inevitable. You will be riding the missile that contains your payload.

## Step 2
## Make a plan.

Elicit the feeling/emotion/ of "what-you-want" and begin to create the steps that would ultimately lead you to accomplishing your goal. The more detailed the better because these details will help you deal with unforeseen events that might happen. Spend days or weeks on this plan if you have to. Detail is important.

By constantly reviewing your plan and comparing it to the reality of your current situation you allow yourself to be flexible to alter your plan amid changing circumstances. Do not get "married" to your plan. Your plan is only a vehicle to getting what-you-want and it needs to be maliable to suit changing situations.

## Step 3
## Link every single step of your plan to "what you REALLY want."

This means doing what NLPers call "anchoring" the feeling of "what-you-want" to any act, large or small, that gets you closer to your goal.

For example, let's assume your goal is to own a new Mustang Convertible. What it will give you when you have (what you REALLY want) is the fulfillment of a childhood dream, a sense of accomplishment and pride. Let's further assume that your current income is too low to afford payments, so you make a plan.

The plan includes asking your boss for more hours at work, finding things to auction on Ebay and cutting back on the overpriced coffee drinks.

The key to getting the greatest benefit from this is *every time* you do some action toward your goal you acknowledge you are getting closer to what you really want.

In NLP terms, you are creating a powerful emotional anchor that you fire off at every moment you do something that brings your goal closer.

The idea is to make achieving your goals, and by extension getting what-you-want, a self-rewarding and self-perpetuating process.

## Step 4
## Test it out.

All this means is to make sure that it works. But first you have to make it work.

Elicit that powerful emotional feeling of "what-you-want" then link it to one thing, anything, that would get you closer to your goal. Do it until the feeling of "what-you-want" comes about whenever you move toward your goal.

The smaller the action you can take to get that feeling the better. Why? Because that is where you will get the most opportunity to fire the "what-you-want" anchor.

Think about it. The small things happen all the time but they will only happen because you *choose* for them to happen. To say it another way, you are choosing to do something that feels good *and* brings you closer to your goal.

What can you lose?

Test it out. Do one small thing that you can say will bring you closer to your goal. Even if it's just a little bit closer. The smaller the better. As you do it, imagine that feeling of "what-you-want." Does it feel good? That is what you're aiming for!

Consider now, that every choice you make will either make you feel good or not. Every choice will either bring you closer to your goal and "what-you-want" or it won't.

Ultimately you are teaching yourself about your incredible ability to choose. Make a choice about how you want to feel and what actions will help you feel that way. Make a choice about what you would have to do **_right now_** create the feelings that you want and do it.

Think what your life would be like if you were to NOT do even the smallest action toward your goal. Notice how that would feel.

## Example

This process was used when I set out to promote sales of the book *"Mind Control 101 – How To Influence The Thoughts and Actions Of Others Without Them Knowing Or Caring"*.

Having already finished the book and publishing it I set out to make a massive sales effort. The first step was to plan in every detail how the process would fall into place. The plan included finding partners to joint venture with who would tell their clients about the book and in return I would offer some bonus material that from them that would act as an incentive for people to buy and link the buyer in some way to the joint venture partner.

The plan was detailed including emails that were written long before they were needed, a web site page, phone calls to various people who would help me and deadlines for every step of the process.

Over and over again the plan was reviewed and sharpened. Only when the plan was complete in every detail would I impliment *any* part of the plan.

Having developed such a detailed plan ahead of time the implementation of the plan was flawless. During a five day period of time I earned over $5000 in pure profit from book sales, my customer base exploded. All of it was done from behind the quiet settings of my room.

The Russian writer, philosopher and mystic Georges Ivanovich Gurdjieff described the human being as a strange being of three minds; the thinking, feeling and doing minds. According to Gurdjieff these minds are seldom in balance. Each mind can have its own strengths and afflictions that leave people ineffective.

A person relying too heavily on the thinking mind will horde information and never have enough information to make the "right" decision.

Someone who uses their feeling mind in excess can only be motivated to act when things "feel" right. They may spend long periods of time lingering within their emotions waiting to act only when their mood deems it appropriate.

Someone overly dependent on the doing mind may appear like a tornado of activity but seldom focuses to accomplish anything.

Since you have read this far in this book, and I know that you have, you can see how each of these three minds are brought into action so that the whole person can come into balance.

By setting a goal and determining the what-you-want that the goal gives you the feeling mind is enlisted and you begin to feel the excited emotions and energies that will move you forward.

By developing a detailed plan toward your goal and what-you-want the thinking mind gets involved.

Lastly, the doing mind is activated by committing to act on each small measurable outcome.

Let me suggest that you can internalize this process so that the thinking, feeling and doing become part of your spirituality.

The author, Robert Greene (to whom I've dedicated this book) made an insightful recommendation in his book "The 33 Strategies of War" in which he describes the one of the ideals of the mastery of warfare as "Spiritualize your warfare".[3]

The same ideal holds true for getting what-you-want. Every step of the process affirms a surrender to a higher power. The thorough planning of each goal becomes a ritual of worship. The binding of emotions to each action becomes a prayer. The effort of each task becomes a holy offering. Each goal, when achieved, becomes a monument of homage.

This process can become your own personal cult of quiet achievement. By spiritualizing this process you create a balance

---

3 *The 33 Strategies of War* preface page xx

between heaven and earth. One hand holds the riches of this world and the other reaches skyward in aspiration.

All of this, of course is sacrilege, because it will liberate you from those people and organizations who are very invested in your bondage and dependency. So, of course, this book is forbidden.

# The Big Picture
# and
# The Detailed Plan

Let's get it into your head right now that you have to have a plan. Until you accept that you need a plan, all that is going to happen is you are going to live an ordinary invisible life, like all the other sheeple in the world and find yourself working for people you don't like and die wishing you had done it differently.

You need a plan. A written plan.

But we'll get back to that later.

Let's talk about "The Big Picture" of your life. This Big Picture goes far beyond your day-to-day life. The Big Picture is like a retrospective of your whole life and how you have lived and how you want to live. Did you take the helm of your life and steer your destiny? Or were you tossed to and fro by the fickle hands of fate? Did you make a choice on how your life would transpire or did the world choose that for you?

That is the "Big Picture" of your life.

As human beings we tend to a mass of conflicting impulses and urges. At one moment we are moved by fun, risk and excitement then another moment we want to huddle for security. A typical example is the conscious desire to be fit, healthy and at an ideal weight yet we may be pulled by uncontrolable cravings and gustitorial urges.

The goal, of course, is to bring this legion or urges and desires under one command. The easiest way to do that is to create a life purpose, a goal, a destiny that will reign in the more rowdy parts of our nature and direct them towards your higher purpose. Like a general commanding an army the goal is to bring each impulse in line with your goals and what-you-want thus creating a rightious military campaign.

But "The Big Picture" is built upon details. These details are moment to moment events that include incidents and your choices and reactions to them. The details that make up the Big Picture of your life pass by moment by moment, nanosecond by nanosecond.

To build the Big Picture that you want you will have to learn that you have incredible control over every passing second of your life.

As each second passes you have incredible control. You may not be able to control the weather or so-called "acts of God" but you can control how you react to them and *that* is your secret weapon.

With the passing of every second you have only two choices: to focus on your goal, what-you-want, your destiny, and do some action that will bring it closer, or to be a sheep that is herded through life by outside events and internal fears and instincts. The latter choice always concludes the same way, with a trip to the slaughter house.

The choice is all yours.

While there is a Big Picture to consider, the building of it starts right now, in this moment. The degree of control and power that we have in every moment is incredible. But as Spiderman said "With great power comes great responsibility."

The fact is, having this power and control is a huge responsibility that most people refuse to take.

Why?

Because it means accepting responsibility over their own emotions and reactions. That means giving up the belief that people "make me mad".

You must forever abandon excuses as to why you react one way or another. The fact is, that _every_ action you take is choice, even the emotions you have.

This fact is incredibly hard for most people to accept, because if they accept that degree of responsibility, then they would have reevaluate almost every part of their life. Given a choice blaming others for things that go wrong is just easier.

### Thought Experiment

Let's make some assumptions.

Let's assume you have actually taken the time to a) set a goal and b) determine what that goal will give you i.e., "what-you-want".

# The Forbidden Book of Getting What You Want

Congratulations! You'd be surprised how many people just read this book and do nothing with it. You're now in the one percent.

Let's' further assume that you "get it" and that you are willing to take responsibility for how you live your life.

Congratulations again. You are now in the .0001 percent of the population.

During this experiment imagine that your closest friend or worst enemy approaches you and begins to "push your buttons," trying to piss you off.

You are now given a choice. The choice to react like you would normally do or to react in a way that would bring you closer to your goal and what-you-want.

The choice is completely yours. There is no wrong decision.

What would you choose?

At this point it would be good time to point out that emotions are _**deeply**_ ingrained within us at an almost unconscious level. As an example, we've all had emotions "welling up" out of our conscious control.

We've all known people who seem to respond with a knee-jerk emotional response. They make mountains out of molehills and scream, "You made me mad" and "You make me feel like crap."

The point is, that even though emotions are deeply ingrained on an almost emotional level they are still a choice.

How you respond emotionally is still a choice and no one can make you mad or make you feel like crap unless you choose for them to do it.

The choice to blame others is easy, because controlling your emotions and thinking of the Big Picture is hard work. And it's much easier to find things external to you to blame for your troubles.

Let's make it clear, it's very very hard for most ordinary people to accept responsibility for their emotional responses. That's why you can't just walk up to someone in a foul mood and tell them they are responsible for how they feel. There is a likelihood you'd get punched in the nose.

But do you want to be an "ordinary" person?

Now, let's go back to our thought experiment.

So you've decided that choosing to get angry, get pissed off or feel like crap will not help you get closer to your goal and what-you-want.

But what do you do?

Here are two options. Both require that you pause and prevent yourself from getting any further upset.

At the point when you recognize anger or "feeling like crap" tell your self "***STOP!***" and begin to examine the situation more objectively. Think of your goal and consider your options. There is an infinity of options available, so don't stop until you get one that is ideal. While you are in the midst of all that's happening, consciously work at being as objective and detached as you can. Consider the fact that there are other people who would respond completely differently and treat it like an opportunity to learn.

The second option is to ask yourself a very simple but powerful question "What would the very best 'me' do in this situation?" Think about the qualities that "the very best you" has, such as being loving, patient and calm, with a clear understanding of what-you-want, a sense of destiny and so on.

Making the process of getting what-you-want work requires a bit of an understanding of economy. Not money and finance, but the cost and expence of being dragged around by ones own emotions like a dog on a leash. The cost of losing out to emotional reactions is usually greater than one might think. Every time you allow anger or sadness or "feeling like crap" to take over you lose your most valuable commodity, your focus and attention.

Emotional balance is important and, like an unbalanced knife, unbalanced emotions have a greater likelihood of hurting the user. To achieve a balance and an economy of emotions one must learn to ***not*** invest their emotions in directions that don't benefit their long range goals and what-you-want.

As an example a snide remark from a co-worker may trigger an argument but in the long run did your reaction help move you closer to what-you-want?

When you can bring those qualities of balance and economy of emotions to bear in the most challenging situations, then achieving your goals will be the easy part.

An example of someone "getting it" in this manner is a man, Jerry, who seeks success in business and in relationships but he finds that he can't seem to achieve the accomplishment that he desired. After some serious soul searching he realized that all his successes were thwarted by his quick anger and a gullible tendency to become easily inamored. Whether it's a love relationship or a business opportunity he would fall quickly into it and over react at the slightest change.

Upon realizing how he was responsible for his own misery he "got it" and began to take responsibility for everything in his life and especially began to focus on his emotions. The result was akin to a serious religious conversion.

This was a bold step because most people felt, and continue to feel, that this degree of emotional control is impossible.

# Back To The Trap

Now you are trapped.

Because you've read this book all the way up to this point you can't "un-read" it. The knowledge is trapped in your head.

To get your goals and ultimately, what-you-want, you know what you need to do and you know that you know it.

You have to make a choice. And even if you don't choose you are still making a choice.

The choice is very clear and very simple.

You have to choose between being ordinary or exceptional.

You have to choose between letting life make the choices about what you do or choosing to direct your life the way you want.

You have to choose between doing what you've always have done and getting what you've always gotten or doing something different and getting what-you-want.

You have to choose between living your life accidentally or intentionally.

You have to choose between being a constant or a variable.

You have to choose.

You can't not choose because you would still be making a choice.

You're trapped.

# Getting "It" and Keeping "It"

Okay, so you "get it".

You've made your choice to live an exceptional life in which you move in the direction of your goals, pay attention to what you are doing and make choices during every moment that keep you on track.

How do you keep the momentum?

The reason that question needs to be answered is because life is dynamic. As much as we can control our life, there are things that we cannot control. Those external events include the weather, natural disasters, other people and their issues.

On top of that, there are plenty of people (you may be one of them) who begin projects with unbridled enthusiasm but, for whatever reason, never finish them.

Suffice to say that you can be assured that *something* will occur that you cannot control and *may* distract you enough to completely derail your exceptional life and while you "get it" you now need to be able to "keep it".

Here are some basic common sense strategies that will help keep it when you "get it".

## Write It Down

Write down your goals. Seriously. Write them down so that they are ready for constant review. You can create a special notebook for your goals or have them ordered in index cards in a "goals box".

By writing down your goals, outcomes and "what-you-want," you are taking something that is merely a wish, a hope and a want, and taking the first step to making it real. A thought and a hope may fade with little effort but a goal written on a piece of paper and constantly reviewed has some endurance and will last as long as the paper endures.

This has been proven many times. Studies have shown that only about 2% of people write down their goals. Those people who write down their goals, as a group, consistently out perform the rest of the population who do not write down their goals.

## A Strategy of Reviewing Your Goals

Build a daily habit of reviewing your goals, outcomes and reasons for achieving them. The keyword is ***daily.*** Like a drop of water that eventually wears a hole through solid rock, it is the slight and persistent effort that makes the difference.

This is no real secret. Consider that when a company begins a major project they regularly review their progress to keep themselves on track.

Have the goals, outcomes and details written down to review, and with them write down the reasons you want them and the "what-you-want" of the goal, the feeling it will give you as you have it and work toward it.

Set aside a time to review and meditate upon your goals and the life you wish to make for yourself. Remember that while your goal may be constant your plan may have to adapt to a constantly changing enviornment. This is why a regular review of your plan is so vital.

## Review Meditation

This is a meditation type of process and is quite effective at maintaining your momentum when done on a daily basis and need only take five or ten minutes. As a recommendation, consider doing it as you get out of bed upon awakening, as it will tend to create motivation to go out and build that empire you desire.

Here is how it works.

Close your eyes and mentally review your goals. As you ponder each goal, one at a time, bring about the feeling, the "what-you-want", that going after this goal will create.

You can use the written goals that you've made but it's very likely that, after constant review, you will remember and know them well.

The objective of this meditation is to reconnect with the motivation that keeps you going. When you feel the motivation you're doing it right.

## Example

You don't have to look very far on a daily basis to find people who have a personal organizer that are either electronic or a more traditional paper organizer.

At the least these organizers are used to compile a daily to-do list in order to keep the owner feeling as if they are being productive with their day. At the best they are used like a tactical weapon of war in which, on a daily basis, they list the actions they will accomplish that will ultimately bring about their goals.

Many an effective manager will tell you how essential their personal organizer has become as a daily tool for their achievement. Their key is to always keep their greater goals in mind (their what-you-want goals) and use their organizers as a tool to keep them focused on what needs to be done next.

## Time Line Meditation

This meditation will require having your written goals in hand and having them lined up in some form of time line from the most recent goal you wish to achieve onward.

With your eyes closed, imagine a time line, a line of time with you standing at one point that represents "now" on the line. There will also be a line of your past but your major focus will be on the line that represents your future.

On the future timeline place each one of your goals in sequential order, with the goal that you will accomplish soonest closest to you followed by the next goal and so on.

Once you've done this in your mind, there are a few things you can do while playing with this concept.

As you see each goal lined up, one after another, you can begin to look at your timeline from different perspectives. You can imagine seeing your time line from above, looking down on it, with each goal laid out just as you've planned it. You can see your time line from a side angle.

You can also start at your most distant goal and work your way backwards. By doing this, you are making the events of your time clearer and more precise. You will be seeing your goals and outcomes in their most logical order and know how the events on the time line precede and follow each other.

Because this is your time line, you can do anything you want with it. You can imagine shortening the distance between goals, thus metaphorically shortening the time between achieving goals. You can add more and more details to your time line for each goal, so that the plan to accomplishing the goal becomes clearer.

Go ahead and modify your time line to see how it effects the strength of your intent.

## The  Question Meditation

To  be different from the mass of humanity is to accept a different responsibility. The responsibility for your own thoughts.

One way to take control of your thoughts is to simply ask the right questions. Questions direct your attention and focus you toward solutions and away from problems.

For example if you ask "Why did this happen to me?" you will be focusing on a) that it's happening and b) that it's happening to you. No where does that question focus you on the solution or anything that is good. The focus of the question is only on the problem.

Knowing this, if emotionally something is not feeling right it is likely because your questions are leading your emotions to feeling bad.

A meditation that will significantly direct your thoughts and emotions is one based on asking positive questions of yourself.

As you hear these questions note the presuppositions within each question.

Question: How can I make today... right now... my best day yet?
Presupposition: I can make to day the best day yet.
Presupposition: I can do it right now.
Presupposition: There is a way to do it.

Question: What is good about this and how can I use it?

Presupposition: There is something good in this.
Presupposition: There is something useful that I can use.

Question: What do I LOVE about this very moment?
Presupposition: There is something to love.
Presupposition: I can find it.

Question: How is right now a clear stepping stone to my destiny?
Presupposition: I have a destiny.
Presupposition: Right now is a stepping stop to my destiny.
Presupposition: I can find a way to link this moment, right now, to my destiny.

Question: What would the very best me do, right now?
Presupposition: There is an even better 'me' than right now.
Presupposition: I can be that 'me'.

Question: What one thing, no matter how small, can I do right now to positively impact my goals?
Presupposition: I can do something, even small, that will positively impact my goals.
Presupposition: I can do it right now.
Presupposition: Even a small influence toward my goals is important.

Question: How can I make this moment a memorable moment toward my destiny?
Presupposition: There is something I can do right now toward my destiny.
Presupposition: I can do something right now toward my destiny.

Upon doing meditating on these questions the mind will begin to focus more clearly on what needs to take place. You'll notice a growing sense of powerful resources. Some of these recourses will be obvious, others will be there as a feeling that encourages you.

## The Meditation Upon Destiny

Destiny.

Think about it. Destiny is the belief that you are *the* central character by whose means something great and inevitable will occur.

Does destiny truly exist? Maybe it does. Maybe it doesn't. But the **_belief_** in your destiny is what will make it real.

That and a good plan.

One of the best examples of this feeling of destiny was Alexander the Great. He was born the son of a king who had expected him to follow in his footsteps but his mother Olympia, who was considered a mystic in her own right, had a vision at his birth of Alexander growing up to become the ruler of all the known world. She would tell him these stories of his destiny and early on came to accept them as fact.

From that point on merely being the ruler of his fathers kingdom was not enough for the gods had told his mother he would do something greater.

Nothing prepared Alexander more than the belief in his own destiny and from that moment on he acted as if it were a forgone conclusion.

As you do these exercises and meditations create the belief in your destiny. How great or how small your destiny is will be completely up to you. Your destiny is always in your hands.

A variation of this meditation can be quite powerful when done. Sit with your eyes closed and imagine what it would be line to have a "second sight" that sees your future just as you want it.

Imagine this "third eye" extended from your current space and time looking downward seeing far and wide all that will occure just as you have planned.

The power of this meditation is to imagine this second sight always present as you interact in the here and now. Using this new sense you can easily judge if your current actions bring you closer or further from your vision.

## Overcoming Overwhelm

Some people who don't "get it" may see a life that is filled with one goal after another and feel that it's so ambitious and detailed that it would overwhelm them. But in fact, the opposite is true.

By doing this degree of planning, there is no overwhelm because everything is laid out and written in a very straightforward and logical order. Once you've done your review of your goals, or perhaps meditated on your time line, you will know exactly what you have to do next and all you will have to do is one thing at a time. Very sequential. Very simple. There will be no overwhelm because you will know exactly what to do.

## Beware Of The Pull of Emotions

When moving to fulfill your destiny the ideal is to do be rational and to not make immediate decisions based on emotions. Make your decisions based on what actions will bring you closer to your goals. This requires the ability to recognize how emotions can distract and seduce you.

Your goals and directions in life are based on your emotions. After all, that is why you chose them, because of the deep appeal and satisfaction they will give you. But the actions toward your goals must be rational and well thought out.

Recognize how easy it is to be seduced by your emotions. There is far too much ease to respond to the immediate whim of emotions. This can be very dangerous because these urgent feelings can quickly pull you away from your goals and ultimately away from what-you-want.

Vigilance and training is the key.

Train yourself to recognize when you are being pulled by emotions and learn to step back, detach yourself, and examine the outcome of your response. A rash response, whether to joy, excitement or anger can potentially seduce you into a moment of regret or, at the least, it can slow your progress to your goal. Even the most positive emotions of love and sympathy can hold a danger of pulling you away from what-you-want.

The process of emotional detachment  is strange and unnatural to most people for we are accustomed to being tossed by our emotions like rudderless ship on a violent sea.  To combat it, begin to reflect on those times you've responded rashly and the consequences of those responses. Within that reverie of memory allow yourself to envision a calmer more detached response to the situation, a response that always keeps your goal in mind. Rehearse this fervently and always look forward with anticipation to the next opportunity to practice it.

Beyond this mental rehearsal the only other action you can take is to invite situations that challenge your emotions. Be like a warrior who welcomes battle in order to face and overcome his fear.

You may find this to the most difficult of achievements but also the most rewarding.

In the next chapter you'll learn a few simple tips on how to get what-you-want from others and, if you want, turn your single person cult of achievement into a group effort.

# How to Get What You Want from Others

So far most of what you've read is about moving yourself in the direction of you goals. This is essential but of course to get what-you-want you must motivate and influence others.

There are plenty of books and course on persuasion, hypnosis and Neuro Linguistic Programming (NLP) and you are encouraged to read, study and apply what you learn.

Let me make it clear, when I say "apply what you learn" I mean go out and use what you've learned whether you are ready or not. An example of doing that was demonstrated while I was instructing during "The Ultimate Persuasion Seminar" in Las Vegas Nevada[4]. During the seminar the participants were instructed to go out and do "lighthearted social experiments" and apply what they had learned. They were told to do it whether or not they were ready. Their learning curve shot up because they were willing to push past any hesitation and test out what they had learned.

Without going over anything you can learn from most books on persuasion, hypnosis and NLP here are a few tips that will help you easily get what-you-want from others.

### Appeal to the Needs and Hidden Addictions of Others

The concept of "hidden addictions" was first described by Blair Warren in his now hard to find book "The Forbidden Keys of Persuasion" but I addressed them in some detail in the book "Mind Control 101".

These "hidden" addictions are things we all need in our interactions with others and they make us susceptible to the influence of others. These addictions/needs influence all of us, even when we try to avoid their effect.

---

4    http://www.TheUltimatePersuasionSeminar.com

## Appeal to Peoples Need to be Valued and Needed

Everyone wishes to be valued, needed, and appreciated. The only alternatives are to be judged or ignored. The easiest way to utilize this need is to tell the person how they contribute to the "big picture" of things and how valuable it is. This is much easier that you might think.

Anyway you can let people know that they are important and how they are valued will work. This is only the right and most human thing to do.

## Lead People

Do not be timid. Be willing to lead. While people want to believe they are leaders it is much easier to succumb to the simplicity of being a follower. People will also yield easily to their whims and impulses and find themselves distracted. They need a leader.

Many will speak of the benefits of free will. Free will requires thought and effort and most people would rather rely on their instincts and be lead.

Lead them.

You are the one with the goals and plans.

You have chosen to take full responsibility for your life.

Act in such a way that others feel involved in your decisions but never let them sway you from your goal and what-you-want.

There will be those who oppose you. They may do it overtly or, more likely, through passive aggression. For your opposition you have two options. You can overtly banish them from your influence or you may use deception and follow the old adage "Keep your friends close and your enemies closer."

You can use your opposition to polarize those around you and weed out others and bring your supporters out in the open.

A great example of leading appears in the area of dating and seduction called "the mini-date". During the mini-date the seducer leads his date to various settings and venues in the course of a single date. The effect is that it makes the seducer the constant amid the variable environments making him more appealing and causing him to appear more worldly. The mini-date also allows the seducer to see how good a follower his date will become.

Use this model of the mini-date to determine who is most suited to be within your circle of influence.

The bottom line is you *must* lead.

## Have A Cause

There is nothing more inspiring and appealing to people than a glorious cause. Having a cause allows people to feel as if they are contributing to something much greater than themselves.

When you involve people in getting what-you-want it's important to wrap it around a greater cause or purpose. By doing this you frame their actions as something instrumental to the cause. Those who share our cause will become your most loyal colleagues and subordinates.

Should there be any reason that they do not live up to their promises don't hesitate to use a small bit of shame to awaken them. Make the shaming obvious but brief and then quickly refocus them toward the glory and benefits of the cause you share. Remind them of how important they are. Your encouragement should leave a much stronger impact than your shaming.

When using shame don't exaggerate it. Simply pointing out their error and its consequences is enough.

Avoid becoming a cult of confession that enlists people to bare their souls with their various sins. This may create compliance in others but it will create fierce enemies of those who become disenchanted with your cause.

## Know How to Recognize Other Peoples Manipulation

To be a leader you must be aware that you will be subject to other people's attempts at manipulating you, specifically using guilt and shame.

Being completely responsible for yourself and your emotions means noticing when you might feel guilt and recognize it for what it is, an attempt at manipulation. When ever you hear someone say the word "should" allow it to act as a red flag that an attempt at manipulation is likely.

When it becomes transparent that guilt is being used to manipulate you a calm undisturbed silence will give you the upper hand. Their usual response is your silence is to try to be more specific with their use of guilt by asking "Don't you feel anything about that?" One option of response is to point out that you know what they are doing "You mean about your attempt to manipulate me with guilt? No."

By shining a light on their use of guilt you render them powerless but beware. Often their only option is to escalate into anger and accusation. Again a calm exterior will allow them to reveal themselves for what they are a manipulative hot head.

Your only way to master this skill of calm detachment around these people is to expose yourself to their childish influence. Once others become aware that the overt use of guilt will not work they are likely to resort to more passive-aggressive behaviors. The same response will apply: don't let it affect you and reveal it as an attempt to manipulate you.

## Pacing and Leading
### vs.
## Pacing and Dragging

The field of Neuro Linguistic Programming (NLP) there is a rapport process that is used by leaders called "pacing and leading". This involves first, pacing, which means to reflect the other persons actions, feelings and beliefs to create a sense of similarity between you. Pacing and leading requires a degree of flexibility in case a person halts and doesn't allows the leading process.

For the person who personifies a living force of nature the counter part to pacing and leading is pacing and dragging. This process is typified by taking the follower from the moment of leading and infiltrating all of their awareness with your intent so that their minds are undisturbed by any other distracting thoughts.

# The Forbidden Book of Getting What You Want

Pacing and Dragging demands passion with a strong awareness of the other persons sense of focus. Everything that you do must guide their attention and preempt any possible distraction from entering their minds. To do this focus solely on them while keeping your goals and intention.

## Hide Your Intentions

While you should have a cause that will motivate people your personal cause and purpose should be kept secret. No one can attack what they cannot see.

## Uncover The Values Of Others

You have invested your time to discover your own what-you-want. When you discover the goals, values and what-you-want of others and bind them to your cause they will follow you to the ends of the earth.

Uncovering people's values can easily be done by simply asking them about what is important in their lives. People love to talk about what is important to them. Listen intently. When you discover their motivating drives all you need do is mention how, by following your lead, they will fulfill these values, but make sure that in fact you can fulfill your promises.

Have them imagine the outcome you describe with their values fulfilled and present.

## Allow Others To Feel In Control

While you must lead it will benefit you to do it so deftly that those who follow you feel as if they are in some way in control. This will prevent your followers from becoming disenchanted.

Luckily there are some very easy ways to do this. Firstly, always give them a choice but make sure their only choices will give you the result you want.

An example of that is a manager who when hiring a salesperson would give them the choice of how to be paid. Their options would be either a small salary with small commissions for each sale or no salary and full commissions. They would further be given the option to change to the other commission structure but they can only do it once. Regardless of the choice they feel they are given control.

## Be a Little Bit Crazy

As leader appearing unpredictable gives you the advantage of keeping people on their heels thus they will be more attentive to your commands and suggestions.

Some people accomplish this with brief fits of rage but there are more positive methods such as creating a spontaneous moment of celebration or acknowledging someone for their achievement in a fun and unconventional way.

When you do something spontaneous and positive in this way people will begin to see you as someone that can create wonderful situations and begin to anticipate these events.

When the act you choose is negative people will realize that you are not one to be tested.

The only advice to give about these "crazy" and spontaneous acts is to keep them spontaneous and unpredictable, even rare. Consider that it only takes a few of these events for your reputation to be built. Rumors of your "madness" will begin to spread like wildfire.

## Play Favorites And Switch Favorites Often

When you have people vying for your attention you run the risk of them competing against you instead against each other. The solution is to pick one person to be your favorite and then, at random times, let them to fall from favor only to be replaced by another.

By doing this you focus others thoughts toward gaining your attention and away from you as a competitor.

The key to using this strategy effectively is in its random application. Like the last tip (be a little crazy) being unpredictable with your favors keeps people off guard. More importantly, people will compete for your good favors instead of seeking to dominate and control you.

A close friend of mine once told me how he used this in his very strange private life. He had several women living with him who would play dominance/submission games. He always was the dominant.

The problem was that these women would create small political infighting amongst themselves and ruin the peaceful atmosphere he tried to foster. Learning from his studies of the Byzantine empire he would randomly assign one of his harem the privilege of "first girl". The "first girl" position had benefits of more of his attention and having one of the other girls serving her.

Just as randomly as he gave the position he would take it away. The result was that their attentions turned from their own internal power struggles to how best to serve him, which was the purpose of their relationship to begin with.

## Appeal to Peoples Need for a Scapegoat

Having a scapegoat for your problems goes against the rule of accepting responsibility for everything in your life. Nonetheless, being able to blame someone or something else for your problems is almost irresistible. Just consider the feeling you have when, in the midst of your troubles, someone says "It's not your fault."

The key is to always be willing to find a reason for someone's problem that is outside of them. This will often be the only explanation that most people can handle in spite of what you may know to be true. Only a very rare person who, in the midst of problems is willing to look inward for these types of solutions.

"You make me feel like crap." and "You make me mad." are the catch phrases of mass of humanity unwilling to take *real* control over their lives.

**Create A Cult Of Achievement**
**"Community of Uncommon and Limitless Thinkers"**
**aka C.U.L.T.**

This step may only be suited for a few but the potential for gain is limitless.

Bring together a group of people who understand the concepts described in this book and be a support system for one another. Just like any good cult or business model there should be rules and a format to ensure that the meeting has a consistent flow.

The easiest way to develop your own cult of achievement is to operate it something like an Alcoholics Anonymous meeting in which everyone supports one another and there is no single leader of the group. Because the format is the same everyone knows what is expected and the results can be consistent.

People have had meetings similar to this and called them Master Mind Groups. The difference between a Cult of Achievement and a typical Master Mind Group is that most Master Mind Groups are only focused on making commitments and being held accountable. A Cult of Achievement is much more interested in the maintaining of it's members personal visions. The achievements discussed at a Cult of Achievement meeting are all refocused toward the individuals big picture.

Here is a sample of how your Cult of Achievement can be run. First the basic rules.

Rules

#1.Keep your eye on the "big picture"; the reason behind all your goals.

#2. No Blaming. No Guilt. No Excuses.

#3. Know that if you can help someone in the group without compromising your goals, help them.

#4. Every challenge and obstacle hides a lesson and an opportunity if you look for it. When you discuss challenges *always* state the valuable lesson you learned.

Meeting Format

The meeting is assigned a meeting facilitator who's responsibility is to maintain the flow of the meeting and keep the tone upbeat.

# The Forbidden Book of Getting What You Want

**Agenda:**
- Meeting begins with a reading from "The Forbidden Book of Getting What You Want".

- Individuals are invited to stand and share the following: their goals, outcomes and visions.

- State what they are going to make happen using S.M.A.R.T. objectives.

- State any challenges they've come across and the valuable lesson they have learned.

- The resources they don't have and invite other members to contact and support them.

- Each person who speaks is given a HUGE round of applause when done.

- Ask who is willing to run the next meeting or who will volunteer for the various portions of the next meeting.

- Final words of encouragement read from any source or author.

- Conclude with Applause.

- Networking.

- Just like in AA, members can seek a sponsor who will help them through the steps and to whom they can be accountable.

## Rules For Being A Sponsor

#1 Keep the focus on the big picture.
#2 No blame. No guilt. No excuses.

#3 Assist the member to go through the process of finding out their goals, their what-you-what and the S.M.A.R.T. outcomes to getting there.

#4. One of your basic goals as sponsor is to help the member create a balance between their thinking, feeling and doing by following the step within this book.

#5. Get a commitment from the member to review and meditate on their plan.

At the end of this book you'll find notes and recommendations on how to start your own "Cult of Achievement".

## Conclusion

Become a force of nature.

This is what leading is all about.

You have done all the work to get what-you-want. There is no reason you should not have it.

Do not listen to those who grumble, complain and give excuses. With these people you have two choices, to turn them to your cause or turn them away.

Become a force of nature.

# When You Really "Get It"

When you *really* get it, things begin to change in your life. The best part of it is that you have complete control and you *feel* it.

Life takes on a another dimension. Your life is no longer measured by just it's length but by its depth.

There is no sense of panic when the unexpected occurs because every event on your timeline is clear to you and you have prepared yourself for when the unexpected occurs.

You feel a sense of destiny on a daily basis, almost as if you know what is going to happen next because, for the most part, you do.

People around you notice your quiet sense of confidence and feel safe in your presence.

With this feeling of destiny and control you will likely feel another feeling, a weight of responsibility, but it is a weight you will gladdly bare because you have given up excuses and blaming and agreed to take responsibility for your own life.

For one thing, when you really "get it", you free yourself from the cycle of self-destruction, the cycle we alluded to in our discussion of the differences between what we want and what we think we want, which is our goals and our true intent. Think back to those celebrities we mentioned, individuals who are clearly plagued by unhappiness. Okay, it's not just celebrities. Perhaps you know a few people who are clearly unhappy, who act out on self-destructive impulses, often developing addictions to drugs, alcohol, food, attention, gambling; just about anything you can think of. Well, when you really "get it", you can bid farewell to such problems.

Think of the likes of Benjamin Franklin for example. Look at the few level-headed celebrities. Everyone loves Meryl Streep and she's a perfect example of someone who is totally grounded. Professionally, she's a legend. She has a family and has avoided the Hollywood classic behavior of marrying only to get divorced. Her kids appear totally stable, unlike the Hilton and Richie clans.

People who "get it" stick out. They are happy. Sure they experience the same trials and tribulations as the rest of us, but on the scale of things, they are happy and fulfilled in their lives.

There are some who believe that one should never get too comfortable lest they lose their motivation. But it is not comfort that you must fear but complacency. Complacency causes one to drop their guard and opens them to distractions or worse, attack. By nurturing a sense of destiny you create a quiet middle ground. You look at the world with a calm and realistic objectivity. This allows you to measure your next action or response by how well it moves you toward your goal, your what-you-want, or your destiny.

Once you really understand what-you-want, you can act with the Intent, the true Intent, necessary to achieve it. Once you achieve it, you too will enjoy that peace of mind and that fundamental happiness that has resonated in the lives of a handful of individuals throughout history.

---

"The self-confidence of the warrior is not the self-confidence of the average man. The average man seeks certainty in the eyes of the onlooker and calls that self-confidence. The warrior seeks impeccability in his own eyes and calls that humbleness. The average man is hooked to his fellow men, while the warrior is hooked only to infinity."

~Carlos Castenada

# Glacial vs. Volcanic Ambition

Earlier I mentioned that by solidifying your goals and desires you can transform yourself into a force of nature. There are consequences to how your ambition manifests. Let's consider two forces of nature that can illustrate your ambition, the glacier and the volcano.

| Volcano | Glacier |
|---|---|
| The volcano shocks all when it erupts in threatening violence. | The glacier seems ever present. No one notices it's steady and unstoppable movement. |
| People will run from a volcano. | People build homes near a glacier and even make them a part of their mythology. |
| People will immediately battle the threat of the volcano. | People sleep comfortably at night with the glacier outside their door and use its waters to sustain them. |
| The volcano is remembered with fear. | The glacier is remembered with respect. |
| Fast and violent. | Slow and persistent. |
| A volcano will not suffer any fool and destroy them in an instant. | A glacier will suffer fools and use their weaknesses in their favor. |

There is an assumption that some people may have when they begin this journey. They may assume that life will become fast paced and frenetic, thinking they will become an explosion of achievement. This is possible but it can lead to burnout.

The urgency of youth may create volcanic ambition, but with age one sees the wisdom of turning down the heat to bring ambition to a slow but consistent simmer.

Let's consider the metaphor of war. War is nothing more than politics by other means. So when you "get it" a battle is only one part of the overall war and the war itself is just part of a glorious political campaign.

A battle can be won or lost, but it is just one battle, not the entire war. While others may run to and fro amid the urgency of the battle you sit on high, detached, witnessing not just the single battle but the entire campaign. Like playing chess you move your pieces like a master always with the end result in mind while the rest of the world is worried about how to protect their pawns.

> "You don't make moves in chess. You make choices."
> ~ **Anonymous Chess Player**

# Excellence vs. Perfection

Being a "force of nature" and living a life of great achievement is not about doing everything perfectly. As a matter of fact, that would be impossible because you *will* make mistakes. To reach for perfection would be an inevitable disaster because perfection is binary. You either have it or you don't. Perfection is comparing your action to an often unrealistic ideal, and as a result you learn very little. Only that you did or didn't do it.

A different strategy is to look at the small progress that you make in pursuit of your goals and "what-you-want". Anything that brings you closer, even incrementally, is noted, rewarded and used as a measurement to improve upon.

By looking for improvements (even small ones) you are constantly learning.

Mistakes, challenges, obstacles will happen so it is what you do with them that will make the difference. From them you can learn just as much as from your successes.

Perfection is static but improvement is dynamic.
There is no failure, only feedback.

A good defeat and humiliation can be one of your greatest assets. While initially these events will sting, understand that by focusing on the pain of your mishap you are avoiding the potential lessons you can learn from them. When these inevitable events occur it's important to quickly shake yourself off, step back from the emotional insult and dissect it for potential lessons.

These lessons from defeat can cause you to reevaluate your thinking, sharpen your strategy and strengthen your resolve.

By doing this you build in a flexibility to events that is more valuable than any long list of memorized rules. Fluidity and flexibility are important because with these qualities you can adapt to the flow of life and events.

As forces of nature, the wind and water do not halt at a barrier but merely go around it.

Think of David Bowie and let his words strike you as the truth. "Ch-ch-changes, tryin' to face the strain." We're all trying to face the problem of change in our life. We're all trying to work through changes during what can be very difficult times. Change can be a strain, yet, when did we decide that change was such a strain, so difficult for all of us to process? For many change is an opportunity.

Consider this because what you tell yourself will help you develop the flexibility that we've spoken of in this chapter. As for the context of perfection versus improvement, if we recognize change as the chance to improve, rather than as a challenge to become perfect, we can start to work through the changes in our lives.

Still, the failure to understand the important distinction between perfection and excellence creates a considerable problem, a roadblock to getting what-you-want in life and achieving any state of satisfaction.

Too many of us make the mistake of demanding perfection. We demand perfection from ourselves and believe that we're in a competition with not just the world but with an imaginary ideal. We demand perfection from others and allow ourselves to become critics, hypocrites much of the time, when people fall short of our unrealistic and unwarranted expectations. Too many people get stuck in demanding perfection from themselves and from others and leave little or no room to allow for improvement or progress of any kind.

When we're stuck in the myth that change depends on perfection, on a preconceived notion that success must be material, tangible, we are sucked into a viscous cycle.

With time we convince ourselves that one slip up is the end of the world and the end of our chance to get the things we want. As an example, you go off your diet for one night and conclude that you've failed on all the other days and nights before and after. You trash the whole plan.

Perfectionism defeats you in the face of every mistake, every slip up. We try to change ourselves at once because living imperfect, as an imperfect specimen is too much. We have to lose weight overnight, even if it's unhealthy. We have to be on the fast track to wealth, even if it means we don't spend any time with our families. We try to change ourselves in one go, with one fail swoop, but there's no way we can sustain it.

Depression becomes the inevitable result, the only response we can muster to our own heartless disregard of the need to take care of ourselves.

Measure your progress by increments instead of leaps.

Don't fail to appreciate progress. Acknowledge that even the smallest amount of progress is still progress. Even the smallest change, if positive, is positive change and a step in the right direction, one step closer to our goals. That is the essence of excellence.

If you want to learn the trick to getting what-you-want you need to slow down and start to celebrate *every* improvement, even the smallest changes that you experience in your life. Of course, most of us gloss over the small stuff, so it's also time to change the way we look at ourselves and the world. You can do this by breaking things into smaller steps. Doing this allows you to "see all the cogs in the machine" of your life.

Put an end to the negative association you have with the notion of breaking things. Breaking things down is not the same as smashing your mother's favorite vase. When a goal or a proposed change in our lives looks big, too big to accomplish in one fail swoop, it is time to break that change or goal down into smaller, manageable parts. Small is manageable. Repeat that as your mantra. By undertaking things bit by bit, you create numerous opportunities to reward yourself for the progress you make. And progress becomes virtually inevitable.

When you do a little bit more and go a little bit further, each day; when you stretch yourself out gradually and build your strength, you inevitably learn to handle stress better. You learn that there is a greater power within you. This is a power you might have overlooked if you decided, one day, to take up jogging. Try and run a marathon without training, you're going to fall flat on your face well before the finish line. Great achievements don't happen over night. You can't run a mile without training. Take your goal further one step at a time, one day at a time, and recognize the process of change.

Amazingly, most of us believe that once we've learned something new, change will just happen fast and all at once. Rarely, if ever, is this the case. What's far more common and all around us, are the gradual shifts, the four stages of change.

1. We learn a new skill or piece of information. We try something different based on experience but we find still that the old habits linger.

2. We still find ourselves reverting to the old, familiar ways. We catch ourselves in the process of doing that same old thing. We've reverted to our old habits even thou we know that they don't work. Consciously, we stop in our tracks, the old tracks, and try to do something new and different for ourselves.

3. We're more conscious and this time we stop, we pause, right before doing the same old thing, the thing we know doesn't work. Now we're aware, we do something new and different. We give change a chance.

4. Finally, we incorporate the change unconsciously. We reach a point that the definitions old and new no longer apply. We naturally do what was once new and differently only now what was new and different is starting to feel natural, unforced. We are learning a new habit. The change we pursued and sought to achieve is becoming manifest in our process.

The bottom line is that change does not have to be a strain. Change should not be a strain, nor should it be difficult for an individual to deal with. When we stop demanding perfection and start accepting that the ability to make progress is really the truest manifestation of perfection, we are well on our way to winning the battle.

Remember the battle between the rock and the river? Well, the river always wins. Persistence leads to progress and progress is the best any of us can achieve

Another reality about accepting progress is that we finally accept our own limitations. We accept that we don't control the entire universe. We don't create the problems and we're not the worst human beings on the planet. We can start to accept our own mortality, the fragility of our lives as we acknowledge the need to progress rather than to perfect. True change, after all, happens as we achieve self-acceptance, as we progress towards it.

The gradual acceptance of yourself and the world around leads to the realization of the greater spiritual truth: each individual is perfect as they are. Perfection does not have degrees. We are all perfect; that is why we always fail to achieve perfection when we chase it. We're chasing it because we don't see the bigger picture. We're perfect as we are, and everything we experience is part of some greater destiny, the path we are walking as individuals.

As you strive for what-you-want, you need to accept that you are on a journey, that you are, in a sense, subject to a state of spiritual liberation. Accept this and the very notion that you are imperfect, that you have "bad habits" will fall away.

To accept what you have and know what-you-want you need to determine where you are to where you want to be. You need to understand who you are, and accept yourself. Be honest with yourself. Honesty is always the best policy and there is no right or wrong in the most expanded sense. There is no good or bad that we need to detect or challenge in the broader scheme of things. Choose to experience, to progress, or remain blocked and immobile struggling and always failing to recognize your own perfection.

# More of The Trap

**Warning!**
This chapter is about pain.
Just reading it is designed to bring about enough discomfort to motivate you.

Within the field of Neuro Linguistic Programming there exists the often mentioned "propulsion system" that is designed to create powerful and lasting motivation.

To be an ideal propulsion system there must be two features 1) powerful positive feelings that motivate you to go after your goals and 2) powerful negative feelings toward not going after your goals. The result of these two forces are feelings of excitement, joy and pleasure when you go after your goals and feelings of fear, anxiety and dread when you hesitate from moving toward your goals. You are incorporating both the carrot and the stick.

To some degree we have already created the positive component of a propulsion system that is designed to make you go after your goals and help you get what-you-want. You've discovered most of the positive aspect to going after what-you-want.

Let's focus on the negative for a while and turn up the pain, fear, despair and dread if, for some reason, you feel you're already not "trapped" enough.

Let yourself imagine someone just like you, who has read this book and took it as a call to action only to have let it fall away, like so many other things. The book and all its important messages were pushed away by urgent family matters, long hours at a demanding job and evenings of watching television because 'It's how I relax'.

Years pass and this person, who is just like you, looks back on their long life and realizes that there is more years of life behind them than in front of them. The years have rushed by and they, once again, find this book and remember the excitement, joy and enthusiasm that they felt. They look at what they had set out to achieve and how it in no way measures up to the glorious life they had planned for themselves.

# The Forbidden Book of Getting What You Want

This person, who is just like you, realizes their life has been squandered. They had gotten comfortable and complacent and the minutes they had valued as dallors,were spent as if they were dimes.

All that they could have done, they now know, can never be fulfilled.

Looking down at their hands they see all the deeds these hands could have done but didn't. Even their reflection shows a face chiseled by wasted time and indulgent impulses.

This person, who is just like you, battles a growing void within them with rationalization. "Of course, I did the best I could." they tell themselves in a screaming voice trying hard to believe it.

Then finally, feeling calmed by their own justifications and excuses they sit back looking at sky on a moon lit night. They see the full moon and remember being asked once long ago "How many full moons will you see in a life time?"

They realize this full moon, which will wane and fade, may be the last they ever see.

So, I have to ask you how many full moons will you see? Just because we don't know when life will end we think it's limitless. But it is not.

You don't know how many full moons you'll see. Perhaps 100 or perhaps only ten.

How many times will you hear the voice of the one person who means so much to you? Maybe 1000. Maybe only once.

The only time that is important is _**now**_.

When will _**now**_ be the right time to go after what-you-want?

Are you are not sufficiently **trapped** into going after what-you-want? Then consider the alternative.

There is no one on this earth who can convince you to take the steps needed to live a full life.

Were I able to do it, I would. But I cannot.

Only you can do it.

To live the life you want does not take months or years. The amount of time it takes is a single moment: _**now**_.

Only the idea of death makes a warrior sufficiently detached so that he is capable of abandoning himself to anything. He knows his death is stalking him and won't give him time to cling to anything so he tries, without craving, all of everything.

~ **Carlos Castaneda**

# Other Details

## Talking About Your Goals

There are two schools of thought about whether or not you should share your goals with others. Let's address them both.

## Sharing Your Goals

There are those who say that when we share our goals with others we create a "pressure of accountability," meaning, that because we have shared our goals with others, we are putting pressure on ourselves to live up to your statement. As a general rule, it does work to create a measurable degree of compliance.

Pressure of accountability is the type of pressure that is used in Alcoholics Anonymous when people stand up in front of a group and proclaim that they are not going to drink _today_ and that they want to remain sober. This is also why many stop-smoking programs encourage people to tell others that they plan to quit smoking.

As an example, have you ever made a promise to someone that you only half meant or felt only partially motivated to fulfill? As a general rule it is an unpleasant feeling to make that type of promise, but by making the promise you know it will feel worse if you don't live up to your word.

Using the pressure of accountability can be a tricky tactic when you are forcing it on the wrong people. For example, if someone has poor self-esteem and already sees themselves as a failure, they are less likely to make such promises because they don't see themselves as being able to do it. They are also more likely to fail at the goal, just so that they can live up to their own low self-image.

Perfectionists are not likely to do well using the pressure of accountability because of their tendency to set unreasonably high standards. Were they to fail in accomplishing their goal they would tend to learn nothing from the effort and, at worst, fall into depression.

The pressure of accountability does work well on people who have a good track record of achievement. This is because they know how to make realistic goals and focus on achieving them.

## Keeping Your Goals Secret

There is a reason keeping your goals secret can benefit you. Consider the feeling you have when you hold a very special secret. You have something special that is all yours and it's likely that other people want it.

When you keep a secret there are two different forces you must manage, the force to reveal the secret and the force to keep the secret and it's power.

The difference between these two forces is unique. The desire to reveal your goal is one force that comes from getting quick and immediate approval. Consider what happens if you've ever learned a new card trick. The first thing that happens is people will ask you, "How did you do that?" They will beg, plead, bribe and promise just to find out how you did it.

The desire to tell the secret is great but if you've ever yielded to that desire you'll find that the reward is brief. You get some thanks, a smile, and then it's gone. Worse, now your secret is no longer a secret and it's no longer yours. The only way you can gain back what you lost is to resist the next person who pleads for you to reveal the secret. There is a reason the magicians' first rule is to never reveal their secrets.

Sometimes the desire to tell your goal is to gain approval or to boost your ego. But if you reveal your goal for that reason, then it's proof your ego needs strengthening. Sometimes, simply keeping the secret of your goal long enough as you work toward achieving it is enough to strengthen the ego. The ego can become stronger because you are gaining control over forces that are more powerful than you can imagine: your own impulses. Keeping the goal secret is an accomplishment in itself and can be enough to feel a sense of achievement.

Beware of the envy of others when it comes to sharing your accomplishments. Envy is a very primal and powerful emotion to which few would admit. Some people may harbor envy deep behind the facade of support and encouragement. Yet another reason to keep quite.

There is a quote that has deep and occult origins "To Know, To Will, To Dare, To Keep Silent." Many will say that these are the four powers of the sphinx. They embrace the idea of keeping your goals secret and building an internal source of power that comes from intent (To Will). But even devout occultists will agree there are people who will need to know at least some aspects of your goals. These are the people who have skills and resources that can help you. You can tell them as much as you think they need to know and enlist their assistance.

Ultimately, whether to share your goal or not is a personal decision. There are pros and cons to consider each way.

Begin to play with the concept of whether or not to share your goals. You will find that there are some goals that you can share openly and some you would best hold tight.

You are also likely to discover that the same concept holds true when deciding with which people to share your goals. Not everyone will respond to your ambitions with enthusiasm for your success, so choose your confidants wisely.

You might have heard in the self-help community the phrase "You're only as sick as your secrets" and for the most part this is true when your secrets are based on shame and guilt. There is nothing about your goals you should be ashamed of or feel guilty about. That would indicate you are picking the wrong goals.

So consider what goal would make you quietly pleased and proud of yourself when you achieve it. When you have it hold it tight, focus your intent and make it happen.

> "A day without secrets is like a night without stars."
> ~**Klingon Proverb**

# The Direction of Your Life

While much of this book has examined goals, achievement and accomplishment, the bigger picture will show it is about none of these things at all.

Were you to only focus on one goal after another, you may run the risk of achieving all them and saying, "So what?". Many mortal men who have sought the heights of achievement have found themselves in the pit of despair, wondering if there is more to life.

Watch the movie, "Citizen Cain" and you'll see what I mean.

To think this book is about trapping you to be a man or woman of achievement would be wrong. There is more to life than the accumulation of goals just like there is more to a war then winning one battle after another. Lest we not forget America "won" the Vietnam war.

Achieving a goal or victory means very little when it's purpose in the grand scheme of things is lost.

Likewise, goals are only markers of what you have done and sign posts to where you are going. Those who understand this will judge their successes and failures in an equal light. One is no more meaningful than the other.

While the details of this book may be about goals and achievements the whole of this book is about the direction of your life.

Setting and achieving goals is not about creating a standard of living but a **quality of life** for which only you are responsible. By listing your goals, past and present, you should see that each of them is merely a stepping stone that leads you in the direction of the life you wish to build.

To have a clear direction in your life you will discover that there is no end to the goals you will set and achieve. To put it another way, a direction in life is the type of life you want and *how* you want to live and the goals in life show you that you are doing it right. Thus the goals you accomplish will be only markers that show you are going in the right direction.

So in addition to asking "What do I want?" to determine your goals also ask yourself "What kind of life do I want to live?" as well as "What kind of person do I want to be?"

By asking these questions you will further clarify your vision of the future and add more detail to the mission of making that vision a reality.

What if going after what-you-want means abandoning the life you've already created?

Then you must make a decision. Will your decision be based on obligations you've made to others? Will it be based on what is comfortable and familiar? Will it be based on what is safe? There are no wrong decisions at this level, only consequences.

Remembered that going after what-you-want and becoming a force of nature is not a path for the timid or the hesitant. By being clear about what-you-want and the path to your goals you are already above the mass of humanity. Your only step is to commit to it and make it your Intent.

With your Intent now in place neither the winds nor the waters nor the wills of man can get in your way.

> "My purpose and direction are so clear that people in my life have only a few options. They can help. They can fall away and ignore me. Or they can watch it all transpire around me. God forgive the person who stands in my way."
>
> ~ **Darlo Okasi**

# More On The Big Picture

In the 1970's and 80's there was a massive emergence of personal development seminars like 'est', LifeSpring, and others. One of the originators of the est and Landmark Forum seminars, Werner Erhard, describes in glowing depth how great it is to create your own reality and to be completely accountable/responsible for your own life. What he never reveals is the process you can use to get there. Erhart was know for calling the participants "assholes" and tell them they probably wouldn't "get it" no matter how hard they tried. There is a simple and a hard part of "getting it". The simple part (not to be confused with easy) is that all you have to do to "get it" is accept as truth that you are completely in control of your life.

The hard part is giving up on blame and excuses.

Erhart knew that most people don't want to give up their excuses. To him they had to be assholes to not see consequences of such an obvious choice. This book won't call you an asshole to your face, but it won't let up on the pressure either.

This book has been designed to show you the process to create your reality, accomplish your goal and be the master of your own life.

The benefits may be obvious but there are sacrifices one must face when taking full control of their lives. Sacrifices that very few people are willing to show you.

By far the greatest sacrifice is the giving up of blame for the events of your life. There will be no more scapegoats. They must be banished. *You can't even blame yourself!* You will have to abandon blame, anger and judgement as relic tools of a former age and embrace a flexibility of thought that only the enlightened and liberated can understand and appreciate.

Another sacrifice is laziness. Giving up laziness for a joyful vigilance that comes from a focused Intent. Laziness is the relying on of habits and instincts to herd us through life. Laziness is easy for most because we were seldom taught to focus our Intent. The only substitute for laziness is a constant vigilance that is based in joy and the energy that comes from knowing what-you-want. Vigilance can also be achieved by living on the edge and embracing the motto "You're either living on the edge or you're taking up space."

Lastly, you must sacrifice regret.

When taking responsibility for your life you must look at all that you have done as a grand experiment. Every action, movement and thought yielded a result and from that result you have learned. There is no failure. There is no regret. You must embrace everything that happens and has happened and determine how it effects your greater goals. From that you can make changes and modifications to your plans and goals. Regret must be sacrificed on the fire of learning.

# The Forbidden Book of Getting What You Want

## A Story

Here is a story you would be wise to read, about an errant god who was cast to earth.

This god had committed a great transgression and was punished by his fellow gods, condemned to live imprisoned in a mortal human body.

At his birth, he was trapped inside an infant body with only an infant's ability to move and speak. As he grew, every outward aspect of his life seemed ordinary, except that he knew inside he was a god. He knew that in spite of his appearance, his family and his upbringing, there was nothing ordinary about him.

He decided that if he could not reclaim the greatness of a god then he would build his greatness as a man.

Every action he took moved him in that direction. He did so with a calm and undisturbed patience, for he knew that inside he was a god. All the time he kept silent about who he knew he really was. To speak of it would only cause others to think him mad and egocentric. As he grew, he accomplished one thing after another. Some people praised him but it meant nothing to him. Others were envious and threatened by his achievements, but he was unmoved.

He continued to live a life of achievement.

On his death bed, he was surrounded by his friends and associates. Their eyes were filled with tears as they saw life slowly passing from him.

One of his closest friends leaned forward and asked,"You have done so much for all of us and for yourself. How can we possibly live up to your achievements?" And in that moment he saw something in everyone around him that he had never recognized before. He saw a light within each of them that was the light of his former life as a god.

Still holding on to his secret and knowing that his imprisonment was about to end his last words were uttered: "Take what is important and live it."

As the light from his human eyes faded his real eyes opened, surrounded by the gods who had condemned him. Smiles filled their faces and they welcomed his return as if he were a returning king.

Without them ever telling him, he knew then his sentence was not a punishment but a blessing given by his closest friends.

# The Forbidden Book of Getting What You Want

## TEN LESSON COURSE FOR

## "The Forbidden Book Of Getting What You Want"

### COURSE TABLE OF CONTENTS

# The Forbidden Book of Getting What You Want

## INTRODUCTION

Welcome to the course introduction to the only book you ever need to read to take control of our life and achieve your goals! Wow, that's quite a statement, isn't it? Still, every word of it is true. "The Forbidden Book Of Getting What You Want", to which this course provides a definite taster, can introduce you to precisely the right kind of knowledge…the right kind of mindset to achieve your dreams, desires, and goals.

But don't take my word for it. Here is a list of the Main Points covered in "The Forbidden Book Of Getting What You Want" and introduced in this course. Copy it down, print it out, whatever you do, keep it handy!

This is the definitive list of what you will learn if you pick up "The Forbidden Book Of Getting What You Want" today and read from cover-to-cover!

- You'll learn there is a distinction between a goal, an outcome and what-you-want.
- You'll learn that the fulfillment of a goal gives you something greater... what-you-want.
- You'll learn that an objective is a type of goal that is Specific, Measurable, Attainable, Realistic and Time bound i.e, S.M.A.R.T.
- You'll learn that by listing all the S.M.A.R.T. objectives that make up your goal and doing them you will attain your goal and ultimately get what-you-want.
- You'll learn that you can also create goals and objectives about how you wish to live your life. Because these goals are ongoing and persistent there is no need for deadlines.
- You'll learn that when you choose to live this way you can accomplish more than anyone has ever thought possible.

The purpose of "The Forbidden Book Of Getting What You Want" and by extension, the purpose of this course is to help you develop a second sight. This second vision will be clearly focused on the future while you involve yourself in the everyday activities of the here and now.

Your second sight will be the rudder that steers you through the politics of everyday life and lands you at your goals.

What now, you ask. Well, either you can work your way through this course, absorbing the tip-bits of information about the incredible content of "The Forbidden Book Of Getting What You Want", or you can by-pass this course completely and move on to the entrée, "The Forbidden Book Of Getting What You Want" itself. The choice is yours. Whatever you do, make sure that this Forbidden Knowledge becomes yours...you can't afford not to know!

# The Forbidden Book of Getting What You Want

## How To Use This Course

Okay, we won't waste much time on this one. How to use this course…the best way to use this course is as an introduction, supplement, or follow-up to "The Forbidden Book Of Getting What You Want". This course offers you some opportunity to fill in the gaps of your general knowledge about the best way to set goals and go after what you want, how to make the most of your own, innate power. However, the final Test at the end of this course is nothing more than a challenge. Really, it's the opportunity for you to take a key step towards the realization of your goals. And if you've taken in anything that was discussed in this course, well, you will pass the test with flying colors and pick up a copy of "The Forbidden Book Of Getting What You Want" for yourself. The best way to use this course: use it as a motivator to get you to read to Forbidden Book from cover to cover. Believe me, you won't know what hit you and you won't believe how much your life can change!

# The Forbidden Book of Getting What You Want

## LESSON ONE: WHY IS KNOWLEDGE ABOUT SUCCESS FORBIDDEN?

If you read through this section you'll learn:
- The reasons that "The Forbidden Book Of Getting What You Want" is forbidden
- That powerful ideas and feelings are generally forbidden.

Why is some knowledge forbidden? Who forbids it? The simple truth is that the word forbidden stands in for a whole load of powerful elements in the world around us that the haves have and the have-nots don't. Many things in this world are forbidden because the powers that be, the people on top, don't want you to have them.

Forbidden conjures up something of a magical, a supernatural significance. It also makes us think of power, since there's things like forbidden love, which tends to be portrayed as one of the most powerful types of love (think *Romeo and Juliet*!) and then everything from forbidden knowledge to magic tends to stand in for power that is really profound, the power to become rich and get whatever you want. Isn't that what magic does for you?

"Forbidden" is a word that stands in place of many things in life that we are tempted by, that we want. The word might almost communicate our dreams, our repressed desires, and our secret fears. Admittedly, one big reason is simple marketing. People want to have things that people tell them they shouldn't. But, that aside, there is more.

Forbidden refers to control, to power.

But then, why should we be forbidden to get what we want?

The contention of "The Forbidden Book Of Getting What You Want" is that, well, actually, you shouldn't be forbidden the things you want and it's time to put a stop to this ridiculous notion. After all, there's nothing wrong with getting what you want. We undermine our own significance, the significance of your own happiness, if we allow ourselves to believe that self-denial is the only state that can truly made a person happy.

The best path to happiness is self-manipulation. Learn to manipulate your situation to make the most of it!

# The Forbidden Book of Getting What You Want

"The Forbidden Book Of Getting What You Want" will help you do this.

So Why Is "The Forbidden Book Of Getting What You Want" Forbidden?

Check out these reasons why "The Forbidden Book Of Getting What You Want" is forbidden. When you read through the book, you will get the chance to review detailed explanations about these various reasons.

Reason #1

The first reason is that "The Forbidden Book Of Getting What You Want" is about nothing loftier than getting what you want.

Reason #2

Another reason that the book is forbidden is that there are people in the world who depend on your continued ignorance, desperation, poverty, and dependence to control you.

Reason #3

The book makes getting what you want simple and easy and you will put consultants and would-be gurus out of business.

Reason #4

There is nothing "nice" about how the information is delivered to you.

Reason #5

The book gets right up in the face of the victim culture that permeates our society.

Reason #6

The information objectifies the mass of humanity.

Reason #7

Using the information in this book will remove you from the others, their greatest tools of manipulation, guilt and shame.

Reason #8

You will find in this book a sacrilege that encourages a spirituality of getting what-you-want.

*Exercises to Get You Thinking*

- What were you forbidden to do as a child? What effect did forbiddance actually have on you? Were you more or less intrigued by the things that were forbidden?

- Why do you think certain knowledge is forbidden? You should have a pretty good idea already, but if you do a bit of research, you'll find plenty of instances in which particular knowledge is forbidden. Look at what happened to people, scientists, who said that the world was round!

- In your opinion, is there any knowledge that should be forbidden? What is it and under what conditions?

# The Forbidden Book of Getting What You Want

## Lesson Two: Goal-Setting, Objectives, and What-You-Want

### Planning

If you read this section:
- You'll learn the basics of how to set goals and make the most of your objectives.
- Figure out the best ways to plan for the achievement of your goals.

Goals, objectives and what-you-want seem as though they are the same thing. "The Forbidden Book Of Getting What You Want" will reveal to you that this is absolutely not the case.

To understand the difference between a goal and what-you-want, you will be asked to answer these questions in as much detail as possible:
- What will having your goal give you?
- What will getting your goal allow you to feel?
- Why is getting what you want important to you?

You'll also learn that the best way to answer these various questions for yourself by setting goals for yourself in a systematic way. You should write down your answer to the questions EVERY DAY to build strong motivation.

As a guide to goal setting and management, "The Forbidden Book Of Getting What You Want" will also introduce you to a very poplar goal setting technique known as SMART.

SMART is used by many of the world's top organizations to assess goals. Many of the most successful individuals in the world also use goal setting.

According to the SMART programs, your goals should be all of the following:
Specific
Measurable
Achievable
Rewarding
Timely

As you read through "The Forbidden Book Of Getting What You Want", take note of what these words mean to you. Why do you think these are qualities that your goals should have? You'll get the chance to learn more about the specific application of these terms when you work through "The Forbidden Book Of Getting What You Want".

*Exercises to Get You Thinking*
- What questions do you think you can ask yourself to determine whether your goals have the necessary qualities outlined by the SMART technique?
- Think of one or two goals you have failed to achieve in the past. Measure them up to SMART. What do you find?

**LESSON THREE: FIGURING OUT WHAT YOU WANT...NOT AS EASY**

**AS YOU THINK**

If you read through this section you'll learn:
- The importance of figuring out what you want
- The difference between what you want and what you think you want.

Let's make it clear: what-you-want is not the same thing as your goal. This is a very important concept manifest in "The Forbidden Book Of Getting What You Want".

What-you-want is what you will get when you have your goal. Your goal is what will get you what you want.

Think about it, you may want a car for all sorts of reasons, but having that car will give you something greater.

What are your goals? Think of one in particular that you would really like to achieve in the short-term.

**Take a moment to imagine yourself having acquired your goal.**

**Imagine yourself in the moment and experience what you think**

**you might see, hear and feel. Make the images big and bright.**

**Now lock that feeling into place.**

**That feeling is what-you-want.**

The point of the distinction between goals and what-you-want is that goals are the best most logical avenue to getting what-you-want.

When you connect with the understanding that you are truly going after something bigger than a goal, then your goals will become more focused and your motivation becomes stronger. Getting what-you-want will be your compass. Your goals will be your map.

As a matter of fact, why not try drawing out your goals. You could try a map-like image to mark the progress you want to make. Alternatively, you could try a simple mind-map approach to identify the various areas of your life into which your goals fit.

Many people demand an enemy to face to make them ready for the effort. For you the enemy is ever-present, as you will learn. The enemy is your own complacence and indifference.

By doing the processes presented in "The Forbidden Book Of Getting What You Want" you can pull yourself from the complacent and indifferent feelings and create both a feeling of passion for your desires and pain and regret for their absence.

The next step is to use that motivation to create a plan toward the achievement of your goals and getting what-you-want. That plan will be composed of a series of smaller steps called Objectives.

You can develop a complete understanding of the role of objectives in the later chapters of "The Forbidden Book Of Getting What You Want" and in lesson four of this min-course!

*Exercises to Get You Thinking*

- Write a couple of paragraphs for yourself about how you thinking you are going to feel when you achieve your goals?
- How will you reward yourself when you've achieved your goals? Think of a couple of ways you can treat yourself so that you further train your mind to serve as a power tool for the achievement of your goals.

## LESSON FOUR: UNDERSTANDING OBJECTIVES

If you read through this section you'll learn:
- The basics about S.M.A.R.T., one of the most effective goal-setting systems.
- All about objectives.

An objective is a goal that fills five criteria. You can remember this by using the acronym S.M.A.R.T., which stands for Specific, Measurable, Attainable, Realistic and Time bound.

Let's look at these criteria in more detail.

The first two letter of S.M.A.R.T. stand for Specific and Measurable. Why is specific and measurable important? The short answer is so that you can know when you've achieved your outcome.

The moral of this story is to be VERY specific about your goal and be able to break your goal down into very specific outcomes.

Not being specific about your goals objectives will probably not have such dire consequences for you, but you can see the value of being more specific than you have been in the past.

The next two letters are A and R, which stand for "Attainable" and "Realistic". Ask yourself if the objective is realistic for you to attain. If the answer is no, then you need to reevaluate the objective to something that is attainable and realistic.

The final letter in the S.M.A.R.T. acronym is T for "Time bound," meaning the objective is part of a time line with a deadline for accomplishment.

This deadline too must be attainable and realistic.

S.M.A.R.T. objectives are all very attainable only because of the meet S.M.A.R.T. Criteria.

Keep reading and you'll learn how to turn the confidence you will gain from S.M.A.R.T. goals into an everyday experience.

Based on this information, and what you read in "The Forbidden Book Of Getting What You Want", see if you can develop give goals for yourself that demonstrate the five qualities of S.M.A.R.T.

*Exercises to Get You Thinking*
- S.M.A.R.T. is just one of a number of different goal setting systems. Different systems work for different people. You might like to take the information in this lesson and try out the S.M.A.RT. technique for yourself.
- You should also investigate a couple of other goal-setting techniques as well. A quick Internet search will probably serve to give you an idea about a couple of techniques.
- How does using S.M.A.R.T. effect you on an emotional level, meaning how would you feel after accomplishing a series of S.M.A.R.T. goals?

# The Forbidden Book of Getting What You Want

## LESSON FIVE: WHAT'S THE DIFFERENCE BETWEEN GOALS AND INTENT?

If you read through this section you'll learn:
2. The importance of Intent
3. The significance of your Intent versus you goals
4. Why you need to set goals that you actually want to achieve!

The word "Intent," with a capital "I," is going to take on a magical property thanks to "The Forbidden Book Of Getting What You Want".

Point number one is that we are considering a goal to be something different from Intent. Anyone can set goals. The question is, do they follow them up with intent? Do they intend to achieve those goals?

One way to distinguish between a goal and an intent is to think of a goal as an "I want..." and an intent as "I will..." but it's an "I will" that includes a very detailed understanding of what needs to happen.

**Intent includes every S.M.A.R.T. outcome and where they lay upon the time line.**

**Intent, when it becomes magical, makes getting what you want a fait accompli.**

We are, however, going to dwell a little longer on the concept of intent before we move on. First of all, your intentions must be aligned with your goals. Be warned, if you do not align these two elements in your planning and in your actions, without doubt you will lose out on achieving your goals. We mentioned briefly the problem that many people have when it comes to goals and intentions. Most people incorrectly identify what it is that they want in life. They incorrectly assume that they know what they want. They try to pursue whatever it is they think they want but their subconscious mind does not allow them to succeed in the quest. Ultimately, our minds unconscious minds are more sensitive to what we want than our conscious minds. Consciously we might believe that a lot of money, women, and popularity will make us happy. Subconsciously we might consider that only being debt free, having a satisfying job, maintaining a stable relationship, and living close to a few good friends is what will really work at keeping us happy and healthy in life.

Think about what it would be like to have both Intent to achieve a goal and Intent to live a certain life-style. What if you actually determined what it is you want in life and what you need to achieve those things? What you will have done is an intentionally designed a life, a very full and rich life, in which achieving the various goals are almost inevitable.

Pick some action, any action, and intend to do. "The Forbidden Book Of Getting What You Want" will prepare you to actually do what you intend to do!

Repeat this as your mantra: It's the fulfillment of the intent that matters. It is unimportant whether the action is practical or arbitrary.

*Exercises To Get You Thinking:*
- Your task for this lesson: intend to do five things today and actually do them!
- Why do you think intent is so important?
- Can you think of a goal that you actually set for yourself and subsequently achieved?
- What was your Intent when you achieved your goal?

# The Forbidden Book of Getting What You Want

## LESSON SIX: TRAPPING YOURSELF TO ACCOMPLISH YOUR GOALS

If you read through this section you'll learn:
- The basics of how to trap yourself into achieving your goals.
- Why it is sometimes necessary to trap yourself into achieving.

Here is the trap: Now that you know what you know, you can either choose to live a better life and get what-you-want or you can choose to just live the way you've always have. The choice is yours and it's completely under YOUR control.

Focus on these points:

- You now know everything you need to accomplish your goals and get what-you-want

Write down two to three things that you need to accomplish your goals and get-what-you-want.

- You know that what-you-want is bigger than any goal and is the sole motivation in life to do and accomplish anything.

Identify what-you-want! What goal motivates you in life?

- You know that a choosing a lifestyle helps you define how you are going to live and accomplish your goals.

What lifestyle do you want to develop for yourself? How do you want to live your life to achieve your goals?

- You know that ultimately you and you alone are completely responsible for your feelings. No one but you can make you mad, sad, or frustrated.

Describe one or two ways in which you might determine to remind yourself that you are responsible for your actions and keep them in mind as you work towards your goals.

- You even know what to do to accomplish your goals, live your ideal lifestyle and become a force of nature.

What are you going to do to accomplish your goals?

*Exercises To Get You Thinking*
- Consider how you're going to trap yourself into succeeding at your goals.
- What do you think is going to be the most important step to securing your goals?

## LESSON SEVEN: EXCUSES, EXCUSES

If you read through this section you'll learn:
- Excuses!
- How to put a stop to lame excuses and actually achieve!!

Let's look at excuses. There are excuses and good excuses. For an excuse to be a good excuse it has to apply to everyone without exception. As an example "I can't enter a marathon because I lost my right leg in a car accident." Were that a true good excuse there would not be an amputee class in marathon events.

Consider that some people, in fact many of us, have a threshold limit of excuses. This means that one single external event would not stop them but if there were two or three or more they reach their threshold, saying that it's just too much for them.

When you reach the threshold of X number of excuses then that becomes the excuse. You can hear it often when someone gives a litany of reasons why they didn't accomplish things. But the bottom line is; their intention was just not firm enough.

Neuro Linguistic Programming (NLP) has a precept that is good to live by. "When something doesn't work, do something different". This make incredible sense yet there is no end of people who discover that if what they are doing isn't giving them the results they want they just do it more and harder.

Don't be an idiot. Set your intent, assess your situation, make a plan and work it. Should any unforeseen events delay your goal then reevaluate your plan, make a change and continue on.

Like any goal and any desire to get what you want, you are going to have to evaluate or reevaluate your life and determine what is realistic and attainable (remember the S.M.A.R.T. objectives).

Hold on to your intent. Know why it's important to you and be unmoved by the "slings and arrows of outrageous fortune."

Here are common reasons for not achieving goals, identified and shown up for what they really are...pathetic excuses!!

"I don't have time! I have too much to do!"

- Plan your time, prioritize your time.

"Too much work! I am lazy!"
- Having a plan that you can work will help you accomplish your goals and maintain a "lazy" life style.

"My health is bad!"
- There are two things you can do that will help if you are physically challenged at accomplishing your goal. The first is to build your resources of people, friends, employees, etc., that you can delegate things to.
- The second thing that you can do is consider improving your health as a goal.

"I'm too old/young!"
- There is no upper or lower age limit for getting what you want.

"I've had a bad life!"
- People often use the past to justify their fears, compulsions, depression and any number of reason they don't go after what they want. Most therapists deal with these fears and addictions with compassion and understanding but for the sake of getting what-you-want the past does not matter.

What-you-want is a reason to live fearlessly and surpass your limitations.

To free yourself from the clutches of the past make what is happening in your present and future urgent, as if your very life depended on what you are doing right now.

There is an understanding that is drilled into every cadet at West Point military academy. When asked a question there are only four acceptable answers: "Yes, sir". "No, sir". "No excuse, sir," and "I don't understand".

Think about your excuses of choice. Develop a response and stick with it whenever you find yourself looking to get out of pursuing your goal.

*Exercises To Get You Thinking*
- What is your favorite excuse?
- Are there certain situations or feelings that trigger your excuses?
- What steps can you take to prevent your excuses hindering your progress?

## LESSON EIGHT: HOW TO GET WHAT YOU WANT FROM OTHERS

If you read through this section you'll learn:
- The basics of how to manipulate other people to get the things you want.
- What triggers you can use to get what you want from other people.
- What you can do to stay in control and not become the subject of anyone else's manipulative efforts.

Without going over anything you can learn from most books on persuasion, hypnosis and NLP here are a few tips that will help you easily get what you want from others.

The concept of "hidden addictions" was first described by Blair Warren in his now hard to find book "The Forbidden Keys of Persuasion". These "hidden" addictions are things we all need in our interactions with others and they are susceptible to the influence of others. These addictions/needs affect all of us, even when we try to avoid their effect.

First of all, everyone wants to be valued, needed, and appreciated. The only alternatives are too judged or ignored. The easiest way to utilize this need is to tell the person how they contribute to the "big picture" of things and how valuable it is. This is much easier that you might think.

Checkout these pointers about getting what you want from other people…

- Let people know that they are important and how what they do is valued.
- Lead People
- Do not be timid.
- Be willing to lead.
- Make others feel involved in your decisions.
- Never let them sway you from your goal and what-you-want

While people want to believe they are leaders it is much easier to succumb to the simplicity of being a follower. People will also yield easily to their whims and impulses and find themselves distracted. They need a leader.

Many will speak of the benefits of free will but free will requires thought and effort and most people would rather rely on their instincts and be lead.

- Present yourself as a leader.
- Present yourself as the one with the goals and plans.
- Present yourself as the one who has chosen to take full responsibility.

.

There is nothing more inspiring and appealing to people than a glorious cause. Having a cause allows, people to feel as if they are contributing to something much greater than themselves.

When you involve people in getting what you want it's important to wrap in around a greater cause or purpose. By doing this you frame their actions as something instrumental to the cause. Those who share our cause will become your most loyal followers and yes, you will be able to manipulate them at your discretion to get what you want.

*Exercises To Get You Thinking*
- What kind of personality do you have?
- Are you considered a natural leader?
- What do you think might help you become a stronger leader of others?
- Do you find that others can easily manipulate you?
- What do you think you can do to prevent others from manipulating you?

LESSON NINE:

FINDING WHAT YOU REALLY WANT AND FITTING IT ALL

TOGETHER

If you read through this section you'll learn:
- How to create a comprehensive blueprint to improve your life
- How to determine what you really want in life
- The importance of testing your game plan and revising it as necessary

In this lesson, we'll run you through the step-by-step process of getting what you want and fitting together your long-term plans for the future...

- **Determine what you really want.**
   The goal may be the thing or achievement you are going after. That will give you a feeling. The feeling is "what-you-want" because it will motivate you to take the steps needed to accomplish your goal.
   An important road map or blueprint to establish in addition to a business plan is certainly one that outlines a plan to achieve personal development. A simple list or a series of statements about what you want can serve as a plan. Regardless of how you decide to lay out your plan, you should look to establish goals in the following areas to enjoy a complete life:

- Your Personal Life
- Your Family Life
- Your Career
- Your Intellectual Development
- Your Spiritual Development
- Your Physical Well-Being

All of these elements should help you move along the road to getting what you want.

- **Make a plan.**

Elicit the feeling/emotion/ of "what-you-want" and begin to create the steps that would ultimately lead you to accomplishing your goal. The more detailed the better because these details will help you deal with unforeseen events that might happen. Spend days or weeks on this plan if you have to. Detail is important.

By constantly reviewing your plan and comparing it to the reality of your current situation you allow yourself to be flexible to alter your plan amid changing circumstances. Do not get "married" to your plan. Your plan is only a vehicle to getting what-you-want and it needs to be malleable to suit changing situations.

- **Link every single step of your plan to "what you REALLY want."**

This means doing what NLPers call "anchoring" the feeling of "what-you-want" to any act, large or small, that gets you closer to accomplishing your goal.

The key to getting the greatest benefit from this every time you do some action toward your goal is to acknowledge that you are getting closer to what you really want.

In NLP terms, you are creating a powerful emotional anchor that you fire off at every moment you do something that brings your goal closer.

The idea is to make achieving your goals, and by extension getting what you want, a self-rewarding and self-perpetuating process.

- **Test it out.**

Make sure that your plan works. You have to make it work by eliciting that powerful emotional feeling of "what-you-want" then link it to one thing, anything, that would get you closer to your goal. Do it until the feeling of "what-you-want" comes about whenever you move toward your goal.

The smaller the action you can take to get that feeling the better. Try doing one small thing that you can say will bring you closer to your goal.

Consider now, that every choice you make will either make you feel good or not. Every choice will either bring you closer to your goal and "what-you-want" or it won't.

You are teaching yourself about your incredible ability to choose. Make a choice about how you want to feel and what actions will help you feel that way. Make a choice about what you would have to do right now create the feelings that you want and do it.

Think what your life would be like if you were to NOT do even the smallest action toward your goal. Notice how that would feel then take into account these three key points:

- By setting a goal and determining the what-you-want that the goal gives you the feeling mind is enlisted.
- By developing a detailed plan toward your goal and what-you-want the thinking mind gets involved.
- By committing to act on small, measurable outcomes, the doing mind is activated.

*Exercises to Get You Thinking*

- Do you have a clear idea yet of what you want to achieve, how you want to improve your life?
- Make a plan; what are the most important goals to you?
- Have you tried implementing plans based on set goals before? If so, what did you learn from these experiences?
- What steps are you going to take to ensure that you make the best possible effort when you implement your plan?

## LESSON TEN: THE BIG PICTURE AND THE DETAILED PLAN

If you read through this section you'll learn:
5. The basics about the Big Picture
6. Why you need to see the big picture in your goal-setting

Let's get it into your head right now that you have to have a plan. Until you accept that you need a plan, all that is going to happen is you are going to live an ordinary invisible life.

You need a plan. A written plan.

But what is the big picture?

- The Big Picture you need to get in your sights goes far beyond your day-to-day life.
- The Big Picture is like a retrospective of your whole life and how you have lived.
- The Big Picture" is built upon details.
- The Big Picture details pass by moment by moment, nanosecond by nanosecond.
- The Big Picture is based on learning that you have incredible control over every passing second of your life.

With the passing of every second you have only two choices: to focus on your goal, what you want, your destiny, and do something that will bring it closer. Alternatively, you can be a sheep herded through life by outside events and internal fears and instincts. The latter choice always concludes the same way, with a trip to the slaughter house.

The choice is all yours.

While there is a Big Picture to consider, the building of it starts right now, in this moment. The degree of control and power that we have at every moment is incredible. But as Spiderman said, "With great power comes great responsibility."

The fact is, having this power and control is a huge responsibility that most people refuse to take. It means forever abandoning excuse as to why you react one way or another. It is incredibly hard for most people to accept this because if they accept that degree of responsibility, then they would have reevaluate almost every part of their life. Blaming others for things that go wrong is just easier.

*Now you've worked your way through this mini-course it's time to put yourself to the ultimate test...*

## WHAT HAVE YOU LEARNED: THE TEST!!

You are now given a choice.
This is your choice, your test.
You have the choice to react like you would normally do or to react in
a way that would bring you closer to your goal and what you want.
The choice is completely yours.
\*       \*       \*.
What do you choose?

# Other Books by JK Ellis

### Perfected Mind Control
### The Unauthorized Black Book of Hypnotic Mind Control

**Perfected Mind Control** is a mind twisting application of hypnosis.

Yes, it is about hypnosis.

Yes, it is about control.

Yes, none of this is authorized.

Yes, it is scary just what you can do when it's used in this way.

The good news is that ALL of this can be done for the good and well being of the hypnotic subject.

Available at www.amazon.com
or www.MindControl101.com
or www.lulu.com/MindControl101

---

### Mind Control 101
### How To Influence The Thoughts And Actions
### Of Others Without Them Knowing Or Caring

**Mind Control 101** is a virtual encyclopedia of mind control for the masses. From the nepharious to the benign, you'll learn what you can do to take covert control of the thoughts and actions of others. You'll also discover that it's very likely been done to you.

But all is fair in love and war and mind control so use it to your advantage.

Available at www.amazon.com
or www.MindControl101.com
or www.lulu.com/MindControl101

# How To Form Your Own
# "Cult of Achievement"
# Support Group

To form your own support group based on the methods of this book you can take the following steps:

**Find Participants and Make Announcements:**
- Invite a few ambitiuos friends to take part in a success group.
- Place flyers on bulletin boards. Include contact information along with time and location of meeting.
- You can make announcements on local internet boards like www.meetup.com

**Locations To Hold Your Meetings:**
- Your home
- Local community center, churches, or libraries. Give them a call and inquire about how to reserve a room. Most will schedule meetings for non-profit groups at no cost.
- Anywhere you can give focused attention to the people attending.
- Small enough meetings of two to four people can meet at 24 restaurant.

**Special Notes:**
- Be on time.
- Keep to the structure of the meeting as it's described. The structure is designed for a reason – IT WORKS.
- Be patient and keep scheduling groups.

Printed in the United States
104075LV00002B/163-186/A

9 781435 703599